Specter or Delusion?
The Supernatural in
Gothic Fiction

Studies in Speculative Fiction, No. 15

Robert Scholes, Series Editor

Alumni/Alumnae Professor of English and
Chairman, Department of English
Brown University

Other Titles in This Series

Specter or Delusion?
The Supernatural in Gothic Fiction

by
Margaret L. Carter

UMI Research
Press
Ann Arbor / London

Produced and distributed by
UMI Research Press
an imprint of
University Microfilms, Inc.
Ann Arbor, Michigan 48106

Library of Congress Cataloging in Publication Data

Carter, Margaret L. (Margaret Louise), 1948-
Specter or delusion?

(Studies in speculative fiction ; no. 15)
Revision of thesis (Ph.D.)—University of California-
Irvine, 1986.
Bibliography: p.
Includes index.
1. English fiction—19th century—History and
criticism.   2. English fiction—18th century—History and
criticism.   3. Horror tales—History and criticism.
4. Supernatural in literature.   5. Gothic revival
(Literature) 6. Point of view (Literature) I. Title.
II. Series.
PR868.T3C37   1987   823'.0872'09   87-6055
ISBN 0-8357-1822-0 (alk. paper)

When we suppose the world of daily life to be invaded by something other, we are subjecting either our conception of daily life or our conception of that other, or both, to a new test. We put them together to see how they will react. If it succeeds, we shall come to think, and feel, and imagine more accurately, more richly, more attentively, either about the world which is invaded or about that which invades it, or about both.

C. S. Lewis, "The Novels of Charles Williams"

"The Bleeding Nun"
(From a French translation of Matthew G. Lewis' The Monk [Le Moine. *Paris: Maradan, 1801–2*]*)*

Contents

Acknowledgments

I am indebted to Professors Robert Folkenflik, Robert Newsom, and Albert Wlecke, of the University of California, Irvine, for their guidance and criticism during the preparation of this book.

I am grateful to the Nimitz Library of the United States Naval Academy for the use of its resources. I also thank the personnel of the Anne Arundel County public library system for their consistently patient helpfulness in obtaining materials for me.

I owe particular gratitude to Professor Devendra P. Varma, of Dalhousie University, Halifax, Nova Scotia, who first introduced me to the field of Gothic studies. Similar gratitude is due to all the authors, living and dead, mentioned in this book, as well as countless others in this field whose works have thrilled and challenged me over the years.

I also thank my husband, Leslie R. Carter, Commander, United States Navy, for the emotional and financial support without which this endeavor could not have been undertaken.

Introduction

A vision of a ghost is a very different experience for a person who believes in spirits and one who does not. The latter must either revise his entire world view or consider himself the victim of a hoax or illusion—or worse, madness. Modern tales of the supernatural are addressed to the skeptic, not the believer. My object is to analyze several Gothic romances in which the reality of the supernatural is called into question by one or more of the characters. Proceeding on the hypothesis that narrative method can be correlated with content in certain definable ways, I am attempting to show how in these tales mediated narrative foregrounds the problematic nature of the reported events. By "mediated narrative" I mean the narration of an event that comes to the reader's knowledge through indirect means rather than through the voice of the primary third-person or first-person narrator. Mediated narrative may be classified as either oral or written. The first group comprises stories told by characters to the primary narrator or to other characters. The second group includes documents such as manuscripts, letters, or news articles, introduced by the narrator or a character. I call these narratives "mediated" or "indirect" because the primary narrator (who may assume the role of "editor," present only in a frame) does not speak from his own direct experience, but transmits someone else's story. Unmediated narrative, in contrast, is presented as direct address from the primary narrator to the reader in the "real" world. Limited points of view and interpolated narratives emphasize the subjectivity of truth; fact (at least temporarily) becomes a matter of individual interpretation. Preoccupation with evidence and testimony, therefore, often produces a climate of uncertainty. A character's doubt of the validity of his own perceptions may grow into doubt of his sanity and, finally, of the nature of reality. The reader may share the characters' perceptions and therefore their uncertainties, or he may be invited to stand apart from the characters and learn from the inadequacy of their judgments.

When the story's events are presented in mediated form, rather than in the direct discourse of an omniscient narrator (or, in the case of a first-person narrator, at least a prescient one, looking back on events whose end he knows), the reader plays a more active role in assembling the fragments of information into a coherent whole. Like the detective in a mystery, who selects elements from among the available facts to build up a story of the crime, the reader constructs his version of "what really happened." But of course, as Peter Brooks emphasizes, "the apparent priority of *fabula* (story) to *sjužet* (plot) is in the nature of a mimetic illusion, in that the *fabula*—'what really happened'—is in fact a mental construction that the reader derives from the *sjužet,* which is all that he ever directly knows" (*Reading for the Plot,* 13). In thus acting as a sort of coauthor, the reader imaginatively experiences the perceptions of each narrator in turn. He combines these perceptions into a construct of the story's "truth," as the detective reconstructs the truth of the otherwise unknowable crime. Mediated narrative suggests a picture of objective "reality" as ultimately unknowable, and the reader who involves himself in this kind of narrative must entertain every diverse picture of "truth" presented in the story as, if not equally probable, at least possible (within the fictional world).

Doubt of the genuine existence of the supernatural assumes special importance for the eighteenth and nineteenth centuries, from which these texts are taken. These periods are conventionally (and crudely, of course) thought of as eras of rationalism, when ghosts ought to provoke contemptuous laughter. Yet even those, like Bishop Hurd, who dismiss such entities as "exploded fancies" would not reject the supernatural so far as to deny the existence of God. (Though not all Gothic novelists, of course, explicitly confront the connection between belief in ghosts and acceptance of a theistic world view, many do—for example, among the authors to be discussed in this study, Radcliffe, Maturin, and Lytton.) Tales of the marvelous and fantastic are often characterized by tension between scorn for credulity and aversion to materialism. I shall investigate how narrative method sustains and foregrounds this tension.

In selecting texts for analysis I began, not with an interest in narrative uncertainty in general, but with an interest in particular romances and tales. Written during a hundred-year span in which Gothic fiction flourished, these texts represent a wide range of approaches to the problem of belief in the supernatural. (I refer to these works as "romances" in Northrop Frye's sense but sometimes apply the word "novel" in its looser sense of a long piece of fiction.) What sets these stories of the supernatural and preternatural apart from countless others, now forgotten, that may seem on the surface to be almost identical? The appeal of such works is often attributed to extra-literary factors—for instance, the psychosexual insights that can be abstracted from *Dracula* and the lesser-known but still widely anthologized "Carmilla." Yet the same traits are apparent in novels such as *Varney the Vampyre, or The Feast of Blood,* read only by specialists. What literary characteristics set

"Carmilla," for example, above *Varney?* An intuitive sense that my texts, for all their diversity, have a certain quality in common, has led me to identify narrative complexity as that common factor. They share, moreover, a concern with human perception of events at the boundary between nature and supernature.

In chapter 1 I briefly discuss Clayton Koelb's distinction between alethetic and lethetic fiction. Koelb classifies stories according to the author's belief or disbelief in the reality of his fictional situation and the complementary belief expected from the implied reader. Alethetic fiction, while presenting an incredible—though not necessarily supernatural— situation, claims to conceal some truth beneath its incredible surface. Allegory is an example of this mode. Lethetic fiction, on the other hand, is purely incredible and makes no claim to truth or relevance to "real life." Koelb points out that some readers do not admit the existence of lethetic fiction and insist on discovering an alethetic function for every text, however bizarre. Though I make no claims to *factuality* for tales of hauntings, vampirism, and sorcery, I do consider them alethetic in the sense of having *applicability.* I suspect that all stories of the fantastic, marvelous, and uncanny (even the mediocre ones) are read because the problems faced by their characters touch, however obliquely, upon problems faced by their readers. Such stories purport to chart the borderland between the natural and supernatural realms and explore various responses to experiences undergone there.

I maintain that an important use of the supernatural in eighteenth- and nineteenth-century fiction is to provide space for speculation about nonmaterial dimensions of existence, without demanding a positive act of either acceptance or rejection. Written when there existed no univocal social consensus of either belief or disbelief in the supernatural, these stories characteristically use mediated narrative and limited perspective to invite the reader to identify with the protagonist's uncertainty. Thus, an agnostic position regarding the supernatural is valorized.

1

The Fantastic and the Marvelous in Gothic Fiction

It has been suggested that the "Gothic quest" of the late eighteenth century took its impetus from a yearning, not for "a simple succession of ghastly incidents," but for "other-worldly gratification" (Varma, *The Gothic Flame,* 211)—the pleasure of contemplating the hypothetical existence of a realm beyond the merely material. This contention finds support in the romances of Mrs. Radcliffe, in which the supernatural is constantly evoked, though just as constantly (with the exception of her last novel) explained away. The supernatural element was then considered an indispensable feature of medieval romance, which, as everyone knows, provided the inspiration for the first Gothic novels.

The application of the term "Gothic" to this fiction arises, of course, from the eighteenth-century use of the word to describe the Middle Ages, especially in their barbaric and superstitious aspects. In this study the word Gothic, therefore, has two meanings, which must not be confused. When employed by an eighteenth-century author or character, it refers to the Middle Ages. When used by a modern critic, it designates eighteenth-century fiction modeled on medieval romance, as well as later works growing out of the tradition thus established. Horace Walpole is not alone in the belief that in medieval romances "all was imagination and improbability" (Walpole, *The Castle of Otranto,* 7). In the eighteenth century (as, indeed, in the popular mind today) an atmosphere of the marvelous—even the miraculous—was considered the distinguishing mark of medieval romance. The imitation of these tales in the Gothic novel could hardly be complete without "preternatural events," for "an author would not be faithful to the manners of the times, who should omit all mention of them" (Walpole, 4). (Of course, the Gothic novelists were, to some extent, imitating a construct of their own minds.) Considered as pastiche of medieval romance, Gothic fiction differs from its model in its rendering of marvelous incidents by the same "realistic" devices used by Defoe, Richardson, and Fielding. This difference came about partly because by the eighteenth century "the unified world picture of the Middle Ages" had been replaced by "one which presents us, essentially, with a developing but unplanned aggregate of particular individuals having particular experiences at particular times and at particular places" (Watt, *The Rise of the Novel*, 31). Thus it is understandable that Gothic novelists couched their incredible narratives in terms of individual experience (with its perceptual and interpretive limitations), just as "realistic" novelists did their relatively commonplace narratives.

Before investigating the use of the supernatural and its connection with narrative technique in Gothic romances, I shall first glance at the models which shaped the works of the eighteenth-century Gothic novelists. As Arthur Johnston remarks in *Enchanted Ground*, in this period even scholars "wrote at times of romances as though they all conformed to one pattern and had been invented by over-imaginative minds" (Johnston, 11). Johnston's chart of medieval romances known to eighteenth-century scholars provides examples of several tales that may have helped to establish as a stereotype this pattern of narrative "in which the author had given free rein to his imagination in the invention of marvellous beings and wonderful happenings" (Johnston, 9). *Ywain and Gawain*, a version of Chrétien de Troyes' *Yvain* (*Le Chevalier au Lion*), fits the pattern fairly well. Chrétien's tale contains a frightful wild herdsman, an enchanted well, a ring of invisibility, a ring of invulnerability, a magical healing ointment, and a lion that befriends the hero. The characters display little or no astonishment at these marvels.

Such acceptance seems to be typical of many medieval romances. For example, Marie de France's "Lanval" lai (one of the entries on Johnston's chart) presents a lonely knight of Arthur's court, beloved by a lady who seems to spring from Faerie. Despite the lady's mysterious appearances and powers, the hero accepts her love without question. "Sir Orfeo," a Middle English lay that (like Marie's lais) features an omniscient narrator/commentator, similarly treats the supernatural as a *donnée*. Prophetic dreams, a fairy kidnapping, and the benign enchantment of Orfeo's harp appear as phenomena of unquestioned verity. The marvels in Malory's familiar compendium of Arthurian romance also lie on a level with the more mundane elements of the action. Arthur accepts his dream of the dead Gawayne with the same confidence in its reliability as Orfeo does his wife's portentous dream. And in *The Faerie Queene* (to the eighteenth century, the epitome of romance) the "commonplace" quality of marvelous events needs no belaboring. Omniscient narrative and unproblematized supernatural phenomena seem to go together in the majority of well-known medieval romances.

Upon turning to the Gothic romances of the eighteenth and nineteenth centuries, we immediately notice that most of them do not conform to the prototype in this respect. The typical Gothic novel leaves the reality of its supernatural events in doubt for most of the story, in the characters' perception and often in the reader's. From medieval romance Gothic novelists adopted a typical setting, a cast of character types, and an atmosphere of the marvelous, elements which they combined so as to evoke supernatural terror. But eighteenth-century Gothic characters, in contrast to most of their medieval prototypes, tend to be preoccupied with questioning the ontological status of their "supernatural" experiences. A similar preoccupation typifies their descendants, nineteenth- and twentieth-century works growing out of the Gothic tradition that utilize, in an atmosphere of terror, one or more of its distinguishing motifs—the haunted edifice, the sublime setting, and that characteristically Gothic phenomenon, the alienated villain-hero.

Treatment of the supernatural in these novels can often be classified as belonging to Tzvetan Todorov's category of the "fantastic." In this fictional mode the reality of the story's supernatural phenomena hangs in question. The medieval tales, on the other hand, belong to Todorov's "marvelous," in which normally incredible happenings are accepted as fact. In this respect the stories we have mentioned resemble fairy tales, about which Todorov observes: "The supernatural events in fairy tales provoke no surprise: neither a hundred years' sleep, nor a talking wolf, nor the magical gifts of the fairies" (Todorov, *The Fantastic,* 54). Todorov's third category, the "uncanny," comprises works in which eerie events receive natural explanations. He distinguishes "within the literary Gothic, two tendencies: that of the supernatural explained (the 'uncanny'), as it appears in the novels of Clara Reeves [*sic*] and Ann Radcliffe; and that of the supernatural accepted (the 'marvelous'), which is characteristic of the works of Horace Walpole, M. G. Lewis, and Maturin" (Todorov, *The Fantastic,* 41–42). *The Castle of Otranto* is clearly an instance of the pure marvelous. Walpole's well-known "attempt to blend the two kinds of romance, the ancient and the modern" succeeds in following the example of the "ancient" in this regard. The gigantic helmet that crushes Conrad is greeted with "horror" and "surprise" (Walpole, *The Castle of Otranto,* 7, 16), but with no more incredulity than the apparition of the Grail in Malory or the fairy knights in "Sir Orfeo."

Todorov makes it plain that the fantastic, as he defines it, shades into the two adjacent genres of the uncanny and the marvelous and in fact "may evaporate at any moment" (Todorov, *The Fantastic,* 41). The three conditions that define the fantastic help to explain what Todorov considers its evanescence.

> First, the text must oblige the reader to consider the world of the characters as a world of living persons and to hesitate between a natural and a supernatural explanation of the events described. Second, this hesitation may also be experienced by a character; thus the reader's role is so to speak entrusted to a character, and at the same time the hesitation is represented, it becomes one of the themes of the work.... Third, the reader must ... reject allegorical as well as "poetic" interpretations. (Todorov, *The Fantastic,* 33)

The very word "hesitation" implies a suspense that may be resolved, and in fact usually is resolved, whether in the direction of the marvelous or of the uncanny. As Todorov himself acknowledges, examples of the pure fantastic are rare; he therefore employs the hybrid terms "fantastic-uncanny" and "fantastic-marvelous" (Todorov, *The Fantastic*, 44). The pure fantastic seems to be extremely rare in the eighteenth century and somewhat less so in the nineteenth. Todorov's two purest examples of the "ambiguity of the fantastic" (Todorov, *The Fantastic*, 40), Potocki's *Saragossa Manuscript* and Nerval's *Aurelia*, belong to the later period. Todorov also mentions Poe's "The Black Cat" (and I would include some of Poe's other works, such as "The Fall of the House of Usher"). Another novel that we might place in the realm of the fantastic is *Wuthering Heights*, its pervasive hints neither confirming nor dispelling Heathcliff's demonic origin and Catherine's survival after death. Brontë perfectly maintains the delicate balance between the natural and supernatural reading of events.

Several commentators on narratology and on the supernatural in fiction have introduced modifications of Todorov's concepts. Rosemary Jackson, though relying heavily on Todorov's categories, considers his treatment deficient because of its neglect of social, economic, and political factors. Neglect of psychoanalytic applications, in particular, she considers Todorov's principal oversight. The fantastic, for Jackson, expresses forbidden desires in both senses of the word "expression"—manifestation and expulsion. The history of this literary mode, she says, "is one of progressive internalization and recognition of fears as generated by the self." She emphasizes the prevalence of the literary fantastic in the nineteenth century, "at precisely that juncture when a supernatural 'economy' of ideas was slowly giving way to a natural one," when "the fantastic began to hollow out the 'real' world, making it strange" (Jackson, *Fantasy: The Literature of Subversion*, 4, 24, 25).

Tobin Siebers, using anthropological insights to elucidate the uses of superstition in social interaction as well as fiction, suggests that superstition has characteristically been employed as an instrument of exclusion. The chief use of superstition (not the same as, but relevant to, my uses of the supernatural) is to justify the expulsion of a "different" individual, "the superstitious doubting of another's humanity" (Siebers, *The Romantic Fantastic*, 34). Linking the act of exclusion to Todorov's fantastic, the genre of hesitation, he says:

> The Latin *superstitio* means to stand paralyzed with fear over a person or object. In short, the superstitious person is the one who hesitates.... Hesitation constitutes a symbolic activity, in which individuals of the same group mark one another as different. It is a form of accusation that effects social differentiation. Although Rational skepticism and superstitious accusation are of different orders, both reproduce the structure of exclusion proper to the logic of superstition. (Siebers, 34)

We may apply this principle to our texts by replacing the term "exclusion" with the broader term "isolation," whether externally inflicted or self-chosen. The madman, the occult experimenter, the experimental subject, the sorcerer, the victim of conspiracy, and the victim of supernatural forces all suffer isolation. The Radcliffe heroine, in her role as innocent victim, suffers isolation amid hostile surroundings at the mercy of people who deny her the justice of her claims. Protagonists of later Gothic fiction, especially in the Romantic period, are more likely than Radcliffe's characters to bring exclusion upon themselves. Caleb Williams, for instance, provokes his own expulsion by his willful persistence in meddling with his master's guilty secret. Melmoth the Wanderer and Frankenstein invite exclusion by their delving into forbidden knowledge. Victorian characters seem particularly susceptible to the problem of belief in the supernatural when the world denies it (for example, the heroes of *Dracula*). Whatever the various causes, all are alienated from human society. Because of this alienation, their testimony is apt to be disbelieved, and they may be treated as criminals. The "fantastic" situation arises in a milieu where a common standard of evidence and belief is not universally accepted.

The first Gothic novel, *The Castle of Otranto* (1764)—discounting, for the moment, its eighteenth-century editorial frame—is set in a world where such a common standard does exist; all the characters accept the possibility of supernatural intervention in everyday life. Todorov therefore classifies Walpole's tale as "marvelous." One critic, Maria Tater, however, attempts to reinterpret *Otranto* as uncanny by combining Todorov's concept of that term with Freud's. Tater suggests that Walpole "grafted a Gothic tale of superstitious fear on what was potentially a psychological thriller" (Tater, "The Houses of Fiction," 173). This argument, though, skirts the sharp differences between Todorov's uncanny and Freud's. The former, to begin with, is a literary category, while the latter refers primarily to everyday experience and only secondarily to literature. Freud defines the uncanny as "something which is secretly familiar, which has undergone repression and then returned from it" (Freud, "The Uncanny," 17: 245). Some instances of this phenomenon that would produce uncanny feelings in real life, however, do not have that effect in fiction. The effect is usually absent in "poetic" contexts such as fairy tales or Shakespeare's plays but becomes prominent "as soon as the writer pretends to move in the world of common reality." In this situation the writer characteristically "can keep us in the dark for a long time about the precise nature of the presuppositions on which his world is based" (Freud, 17: 250, 251). Freud's uncanny, thus, is much closer to Todorov's fantastic than to the latter's uncanny. Freud's uncanny and Todorov's fantastic both foreground the dissonance produced by the intrusion of strange events into a familiar, realistic setting.

Robert Newsom characterizes the operation of Freud's uncanny in fiction (specifically, in *Bleak House)* as a "tension... between two quite different frames of reference, the commonsensical and rationalistic view of scientific skepticism on the one hand, and the primitive belief in the supernatural on the other" (Newsom, *Dickens on the Romantic Side of Familiar Things,* 66). This tension turns out to epitomize "an imaginative project central in all novels"; the novel characteristically plays off its "empirical or realistic" tendencies against its "romantic or fictional" tendencies (Newsom, 149, 142). In doing so it often "makes reality strange" (Newsom, 15), in a manner similar, we may note, to the strangeness in the commonplace characteristic of Wordsworth's contribution to *Lyrical Ballads.* Walpole's "attempt to blend the two kinds of romance, the ancient and the modern," turns out to be a quintessentially novelistic enterprise, with its ancient aspects embodying romantic tendencies and its modern aspects, empirical or realistic tendencies (Walpole, 7). We may expect to find similar strategies in his eighteenth-century Gothic successors.

Why, then, should we not devote a chapter to *The Castle of Otranto,* universally recognized as the first Gothic novel? Walpole's romance is markedly similar to Radcliffe's *Gaston de Blondeville.* Each book introduces an ostensibly medieval tale with the remarks of a modern "editor." The central plot of each concerns a ghost whose mission is to avenge a hidden crime, and in both cases the ghost's genuineness (within its own story) is vindicated. In both books, therefore, frame and main narrative pose a contrast between two different ages, one skeptical and the other credulous of the supernatural. Why do I deal with *Gaston* while virtually passing over *Otranto?* Though both use the device of an editor to distance author and audience from the superstitious beliefs held by the characters, Radcliffe's frame is both longer and more complex than Walpole's. The editor of *Otranto,* present only in a three-page introduction and thereafter forgotten, displays admiration for the medieval "author's" literary skill but contempt for his character. The fictitious author is conjectured to be an "artful priest" who "might avail himself of his abilities as an author to confirm the populace in their ancient errors and superstitions" (Walpole, 3). The introductory frame of *Gaston* is a story in itself, within which the editor of the medieval manuscript is a character. In this novel we are confronted not only by the medieval author's beliefs, his characters' beliefs, and the modern editor's reflections thereon, but also with the frame narrator's attitude toward the fictitious editor. The interplay among these different world views gives *Gaston* elements of the fantastic absent from Walpole's more straightforward romance of spectral vengeance.

Todorov places Matthew G. Lewis' *The Monk* (1796) with *Otranto* in the category of the pure marvelous. For the most part, according to Todorov's own terms, this classification is accurate. While the monk Ambrosio does express incredulity at Matilda's offer of a magic mirror (to view Antonia, the object of his secret desire), once he sees the mirror in action he is convinced of Matilda's sorcerous power and does not doubt even her ability to conjure up a demon. His meditations upon this occasion do not concern the existence of demons, but the prudential aspects of doing business with them: "He had read much respecting witchcraft; he understood that, unless a formal act was signed renouncing his claim to salvation, Satan would have no power over him" (*The Monk*, 270). In the subplot, however, an episode partaking of the fantastic does occur, significantly in a first-person narrative rather than in the omniscient narrator's discourse. The abyss of uncertainty opens beneath Raymond when he attempts to elope with his beloved Agnes. She plans to disguise herself as the ghost of the Bleeding Nun, and Raymond carries off the real ghost instead (an instance of the doppelganger theme so prevalent in tales of the fantastic). He does not discover this disaster until he regains consciousness after a coach accident to learn that the supposed Agnes has vanished and that his caretakers know nothing of her existence. He is suspected of madness, another common motif (as we shall discover) of fantastic fiction: "No signs of the lady having appeared, they believed her to be a creature fabricated by my over-heated brain" (*The Monk*, 169). The isolation thus generated makes Raymond more than normally vulnerable to the nocturnal visits of the revenant, who claims him as her bridegroom. Still another motif of the fantastic is Raymond's inability to communicate the torments to which the ghost subjects him: "The singularity of my adventure made me determine to conceal it from every one, since I could not expect that a circumstance so strange should gain credit" (*The Monk*, 172). As soon as Raymond's ordeal is ended by the intervention of the Wandering Jew, the story reenters the mode of the marvelous. (It is interesting that Raymond's uncle, a Cardinal, has only to hear the young man's tale in order readily to identify the mysterious stranger—as if a traveler might as likely meet the Wandering Jew as any other celebrity.) Lucifer's final appearance to snatch Ambrosio out of his death-cell is presented as a phenomenon as real as the walls around him. The fiend even shares the role of the omniscient narrator, as he informs Ambrosio (and the reader) of the diabolical machinations underlying what the monk supposes to be his own freely chosen actions. Though Todorov groups Maturin's *Melmoth the Wanderer* with the novels of Walpole and Lewis, the later work presents a more complicated picture of the frontier between the fantastic and the marvelous.

Clayton Koelb's *The Incredulous Reader* elucidates the difference between these two types of fiction (though not by those names) in terms slightly different from Todorov's. This work deals mainly with a mode of nonrealistic fiction that stands in direct contrast to Todorov's fantastic. Among all the possible permutations of belief and disbelief elicited by a text,

Koelb concentrates on apistic fiction, in which both author and reader agree in disbelieving the events narrated. (By disbelief, Koelb means the assumption that the events of the story would be impossible in real life. How the status of the author's—as opposed to the narrator's—belief can be definitely ascertained is not explained.) Since the incredible events need not be supernatural, the apistic mode is not quite coterminous with Todorov's marvelous, but the two are similar. The marvelous, though, while presupposing the characters' belief in its incredible events, need not assume the reader's or author's disbelief; that is, some tales of the supernatural (the eighteenth century assumed medieval romances to be among them) are composed by and for those who accept the supernatural in earnest. Koelb divides the apistic mode into two subsets: alethetic and lethetic. The former— "truthful though incredible"—is fiction in which the incredible surface conceals some core of truth (allegory is a typical instance). The latter "does not seek to convey any truth at all" (Koelb, 33). The lethetic mode is precisely *not* trying to arouse doubts about the nature of reality, for "the assurance that what is being read is not true keeps the story at a distance and thus allows one to take pleasure in it" (Koelb, 226). This mode is thus almost the exact opposite of Todorov's fantastic. The reader of lethetic fiction

> need not fear that a reality represented by the text will overwhelm his reality and drown him. The text, for all its power to move, remains only a text behind which nothing lurks, no divine or paternal authority that wants to open up the reader and plant in him a simulacrum of itself. It remains just language and the effects of language. (Koelb, 232)

The fantastic, on the other hand, involves the reader's belief and invites him to test his world view against that of the text's narrator and fictional characters (of whom, naturally, the narrator may be one). In a work of lethetic fiction, such as *Alice's Adventures in Wonderland* (to use an example cited by Koelb), the reader's assessment of Alice's adventures as incredible is unaffected by the degree to which she accepts them. According to Koelb, this type of text or mode of reading (the lethetic, he holds, may refer to either one) constitutes "a subversive tendency within the orthodoxy of alethetic reading." The "orthodox" mode of reading issues "an invitation to find God or the truth hidden inside the most unpromising discourse, an invitation that appears to render all texts potentially divine" (Koelb, 215, 214). Like Koelb, I focus on permutations of belief and disbelief and on degrees of distance between author and/or narrator and reader. Unlike Koelb's lethetic reading, my reading of the fantastic mode tends to be alethetic, approaching each text discussed as, if not "potentially divine," at least potentially "truthful though incredible."

Within any incredible (in our texts, ostensibly supernatural or preternatural) situation, different degrees and kinds of belief are espoused by various characters, the narrator, and the implied reader. Todorov remarks that "the *fantastic* refers to an ambiguous perception shared by the reader and one of the characters" (Todorov, *The Fantastic*, 47), and one consequence of this generic trait is a preponderance of first-person narrators and "editorial" framing devices. An omniscient narrator rarely invites the reader to share an ambiguous perception. A limited or actually unreliable narrator, on the other hand, is the ideal vehicle for this fictional mode (as Todorov confirms in his fifth chapter, "Discourse of the Fantastic," in which he calls attention to the prevalence of first-person narrators in this kind of fiction). Todorov points out that most, but not all, fantastic narratives provide a character who hesitates between interpretations, a character with whom the reader can identify. The reader's hesitation, in other words, is "represented within the work" (Todorov, *The Fantastic*, 31). To the question of whether the hesitation *must* be thus represented, therefore, this critic answers no; there are exceptions. We might object to admitting these exceptions to the genre of the fantastic on the grounds that our classification of such works would be too subjective, relying on our own beliefs about the nature of reality. Todorov obliquely addresses this problem by noting that the reader whose hesitation is represented is "no actual reader, but the role of the reader implicit in the text" (Todorov, *The Fantastic*, 31). Confusing the two could lead to question-begging conclusions such as Elizabeth MacAndrew's evaluation of the catastrophe in "The Fall of the House of Usher": "Clearly, the supernatural happenings in this story are unreal and so must be seen as symbolic—houses, the reader knows, do not crack open and fall apart" (MacAndrew 196). On this point at least, we ought to maintain the autonomy of the fictional world (even if we grant MacAndrew's erroneous assumption about the integrity of real houses). In several of the texts I discuss, in fact, the unfolding events remain fantastic for the characters after the reader becomes aware of cues foreshadowing a supernatural or mundane denouement. It is the characters' perceptions with which I am mainly concerned. Like Todorov, when considering the reader's perceptions, I do so through the medium of the reader implicit in the text.* Each text usually furnishes internal clues as to how the reader envisioned by the narrator should interpret events and whether that reader should identify with or distance himself from the characters.

In order to reverse Todorov's question, we may ask whether the

---

*The concept that a text defines the reader it "expects" is, of course, central to reader-response criticism. Walker Gibson ("Authors, Speakers, Readers, and Mock Readers," 1950) says that the language of a given text creates a "mock reader," distinct from the real, individual reader, whose role the real reader is asked to assume. Wolfgang Iser (1974), stresses the reader's role in actualizing the text's potential by filling the gaps deliberately left by the author. Gerald Prince's ("Introduction to the Study of the Narratee," 1973) "narratee" is not identical with the mock reader or the implied reader, since the narratee may be an identified character within the fiction.

characters' doubts need to be reflected in the reader. The "discourse of the fantastic" is a useful heuristic device even for texts in which the reader holds a superior position, observing, from a vantage point shared by the implied author, the characters' struggles to resolve the ambiguities of their experience. (Indeed, the reverse situation, in which the reader doubts while the characters do not, seems entirely dependent on the subjective belief of the actual—rather than implied—reader.) A story of this kind is fantastic from the standpoint of the characters, although the reader has the benefit of narrative cues guiding him toward a marvelous or uncanny interpretation. In applying Todorov's categories to my texts, I treat the fantastic not as a genre—its evanescence, in my opinion, makes that term inapplicable—but as a mode of discourse expressing ambiguity in a framework of purportedly supernatural or preternatural events. (To avoid over-repetition, I shall often use the word "strange" to encompass the whole range of supernatural, preternatural, and uncanny events.) Its essence is "hesitation" between two or more alternative interpretations of events. The competing interpretations, in several of the works I have chosen, may center on ethical, moral, and/or ontological or metaphysical issues generated by the supernatural. Though my use of Todorov's categories thus diverges from his own, in common with the revisionist critics mentioned above I emphasize the factors of hesitation, exclusion/alienation, the strange in the commonplace, and the dissonance between the world view of a fictional work and its cultural matrix. Referring specifically to *Frankenstein,* Gordon D. Hirsch, in "The End of the Gothic," makes a point of the way mediated narrative in Gothic fiction allows rapid shifting of "the reader's perspective on events," serving to "open up the book's ambiguities" (Hirsch, 5). He concludes that typically, "Gothic fictions remind us . . . that the world can never be thoroughly grasped or comprehended. At the close they question the reliability of the evidence they have themselves been presenting" (Hirsch, 9). While some of the texts I consider (notably Radcliffe's novels) embrace more "thematizing, reliable interpretation," and "closure" than others (Hirsch, 10), all include such questioning.

I focus on the use of mediated narrative to convey ambiguous perceptions of purportedly supernatural events. Especially interesting is the use of documents, such as letters and manuscripts. The rediscovered manuscript, of course, holds a central place in Gothic fiction, as evinced by Jane Austen's parody of that motif in *Northanger Abbey* (since her use of the convention in parody presupposes her readers' familiarity with the device in typical "serious" Gothic novels). Documents take on an almost independent life, raising questions of their truth or falsity, inviting interpretation by readers or editors. A striking number of Gothic novels, from *Otranto* on, are framed by the introductory comments of a supposed editor-discoverer. MacAndrew suggests that the purpose of this narrative convention is to create "a structure that makes a closed-off region within an outer world." In addition to the frame narrator, she defines the tale-within-a-tale and the discovered manuscript as devices "to make the world of the novel strange" (MacAndrew, 109, 111). This function of mediated narrative, distancing the strange events from ordinary life, certainly applies well to marvelous fiction such as *Otranto* (in which, as we have noted, the mediation is confined to the frame, while the story uses an omniscient point of view). In fantastic fiction, however, mediated narrative performs the additional function of foregrounding the question of the reality of the supernatural. To MacAndrew, the supernatural in fiction is important because of its use in symbolizing "psychological reality"; the isolated world generated by the Gothic novel is the "landscape of the mind" (MacAndrew, 110). I choose to concentrate on the supernatural phenomena as a center of interest independent of (as Todorov says) allegorical or poetic interpretations.* When Koelb asserts that *"all* alethetic fictions may be called allegories" (Koelb, 33), he is using the word "allegory" in an extended sense, to include all kinds of secondary meanings. Todorov, on the other hand, uses the word in its restricted sense, to mean a text that prescribes a direct correspondence between a set of entities in the narrative and certain other entities in the extra-textual world. In the stories discussed, supernatural events make claims to factuality within the text, and characters evaluate these claims by the same standards of reliability they would apply to testimony regarding a "natural" event.

Certain philosophic concerns dominant in the seventeenth and eighteenth centuries (helping to shape, of course, the rise of the "realistic" novel as well) contribute to the form and content of Gothic fiction. In this fiction we often find responsibility for judging the story's reliability thrown upon the reader, whose role is apt to be duplicated within the text by either the "editor" or the implied audience he addresses. The evaluation of documentary evidence and secondhand testimony is therefore a central preoccupation of these texts. The shift in the meaning of science that gave new significance to the nature of evidence began in the seventeenth century. Prior to this period, science or knowledge stood in sharp contrast to mere opinion. Probability was an inferior category falling on the opinion side of this polarized division. The empirical philosophy that arose in the seventeenth century and dominated educated thought thereafter, as Barbara Shapiro shows in *Probability and Certainty in Seventeenth-Century England,* recognized several degrees of certainty—a continuum from mere plausibility through probability, moral certainty, and compelled assent (as by mathematical demonstration), to

---

*By the word "poetic" Todorov refers to supernatural imagery not intended to be read as representational. In a statement like Tennyson's "My heart would hear her and beat / Had I lain for a century dead," the question of factuality, even within the world of the text, does not arise.

infallible knowledge. In the acquisition and analysis of empirical data, accurate observation was obviously of first importance (Shapiro, 15). But since no natural philosopher could possibly experience every datum with his own senses, reliable criteria for evaluating secondhand testimony were essential. The concern with evidence pervaded not only natural philosophy but history, religion, and law. All these fields were required to "assess the credibility of testimony" and "sought a middle way between skepticism and dogmatism . . . that refused to go beyond what the available data and tools of analysis would yield, but also refused to fall into despair over the limits imposed by the incompleteness of these data and tools" (Shapiro, 272). In the quest for moral certainty beyond reasonable doubt, the reports of witnesses had to be evaluated according to criteria such as whether the witnesses were reputable, consistent, impartial, or biased, and whether they were in a position to have the knowledge they claimed to have. The issue of the reliability of evidence carried over into fiction, where the illusion of credible testimony promoted verisimilitude. It is not surprising that the "new approach to questions of evidence and proof . . . this probabilistic empiricism" (Shapiro, 12) found expression in tales of the supernatural as well as more "realistic" fiction.

The empirical approach, of course, depends on trust in the testimony of the senses, and their fallibility was never denied. Acceptance of sense perception as valid must ultimately be an act of faith. David Hume reminds us, " 'Tis impossible upon any system to defend either our understanding or senses; and we but expose them farther when we endeavour to justify them in that manner" (Hume, *A Treatise of Human Nature,* 218). In most situations errors in sense perception are discoverable, but in the case of madness "there is no means of distinguishing between truth and falsehood. . . . Every chimera of the brain is as vivid and intense as any of those inferences, which we formerly dignify'd with the name of conclusions concerning matters of fact, and sometimes as the present impressions of the senses" (Hume, 123). It is little wonder that madness so often infects the protagonists of fantastic fiction. Foucault holds that in the late eighteenth century "the fear of madness grew at the same time as the fear of unreason" (Foucault, *Madness and Civilization,* 211). The culture's defense against this threat was to confine the mad, lest insanity break its bounds and infect the whole society. The response to madness was exclusion. Tobin Siebers' study of superstition as an instrument of exclusion, already mentioned, also points out the similarity of superstition to madness in this regard.

The new philosophy's quest for the rational and the universally valid included the project of discovering a set of religious truths attainable by reason alone and therefore accessible to all people, not dependent on special revelation. This questioning of the necessity for biblical revelation entailed a challenge to the supernatural, trans-rational aspects of Christianity. When the supernatural in the "higher" sense (miracles, special providences, and revelation) came under attack, the "lower" supernatural (e.g., hauntings and witchcraft) came to seem untenable. Conversely, instances of the latter were often used to buttress belief in the former.* I deal with this connection in more detail in chapter 2.

These dominant concerns of the period are reflected in several phenomena found consistently throughout our texts. The interest in testimony, documentation, and evidential proof leads to narrative forms conducive to the exploration of ambiguities in the factual or moral status of strange events. The possible relativity of good and evil is a topic common to many of these tales. Other themes and motifs that seem characteristic of the fantastic mode (as embodied in these texts) are incommunicable secrets, baffling lacunae, madness, isolation and alienation, and the doppelganger—a uniquely appropriate metaphor for strangeness in the commonplace, for what can be more familiar than one's own image? Distance, a condition predisposing to strangeness, is almost a defining trait of the Gothic; the reader is transported to a former age, a foreign land, or both. Temporal displacement is another device almost obligatory in this genre. If the tale itself is not set in the past with a contemporary frame, as several of our earlier texts are, it relies heavily on flashbacks and other distortions of time–sequence to create its effects. All our texts are in some degree documentary fictions; even Radcliffe's novels are framed by the remarks of an editor mediating someone else's report. This editor pose, so characteristic of Gothic fiction, performs two contradictory functions, pulling the reader in opposite directions. First, it confers greater "realism" on the story by giving the impression of a secondary world, discovered rather than constructed. Second, it allows the author-as-editor to disclaim responsibility for statements made in the main text, thus foregrounding the possible unreliability of the internal narrator. As we have noted, final responsibility for evaluating the status of ostensibly supernatural events thus becomes the reader's. Moreover, even with the advantage of standing outside the text, in some cases the reader cannot reach a final

---

*See *Religion and the Decline of Magic,* by Keith Thomas, for extended treatment of the interrelations between religion and superstition in the seventeenth and eighteenth centuries. Thomas points out that even after the Reformation these belief systems were not distinct and opposed world views; in fact, the rise of secularism contributed to a counterbalancing resurgance of interest, among religious thinkers, in the spectral realm. R. D. Stock's *The Holy and the Daemonic* discusses the role of the numinous—the nonrational or suprarational component of religion—in this era, including the way those who opposed the rationalization of religion turned to the demonic and miraculous to support their position. Another work, D. P. Walker's *Decline of Hell,* explores the confrontation between rationalists and supernaturalists on a more restricted issue, the problem of eternal torment.

determination of what is true in the invented world. In texts where even the fictitious editor proves incompletely reliable, the reader must maintain a posture of agnosticism, as in Todorov's pure fantastic.

The term "supernatural" is equivocal, bearing at least two senses. First, it refers to the doctrine that the material universe, nature, is not the only or ultimate reality, that there exists a spiritual realm equally real or even more real. This doctrine may or may not be accompanied by a belief in "lower" supernatural phenomena, such as immaterial entities who intervene in mundane affairs to help or harm ordinary people. Each of our texts, in its own way, uses the ostensible supernatural in the narrower sense—ghosts, demons, sorcerers, or vampires—to confirm, amplify, or alter the characters' attitudes toward the supernatural in general, the spiritual realm. In the typical fantastic situation, the character whose beliefs about the nature of reality differ from the majority view suffers the doubts of others (whose skepticism represents, within the fiction, the presumed skepticism of the reader) and possibly self-doubt. We may note that such fiction could not have been written in earlier periods, when the existence of the supernatural was universally accepted. The modern ghost story is addressed to a reader skeptical about ghosts.

Authors' and readers' understanding of supernatural and preternatural of course changes over time, as do the uses to which the various themes and motifs characteristic of the fantastic mode are put. In later decades the convention of a rediscovered medieval tale largely drops out of most Gothic fiction. While the pattern of distancing the action by setting it in the past does not disappear, in Victorian fiction the past involved is more often the characters' own than some remoter period. Spatial distance (i.e., setting the story in a foreign country or a remote district of the characters' native land) tends to supplant temporal distance. But in such circumstances spatial distance can become a form of temporal distance, as the protagonist moves into an isolated place where customs of an earlier age survive (as in the opening chapters of *Dracula* or in Le Fanu's "Carmilla"). In such a milieu the contemporary character is detached from the customary support of those who share his belief system, and the supernatural becomes more credible. The connection between supernatural themes and the religious concerns of the day remains, but in the nineteenth century the focus shifts from the interaction between supernaturalism and the new philosophy to that between supernaturalism and science. (In a strict scientific-materialistic concept of the universe, of course, there can be no supernatural, since nature comprises all of reality. One would have to speak instead of the preternatural, that which lies beyond nature as currently fathomed.) Walpole's project of combining ancient and modern romances survives in Gothic fiction's characteristic juxtaposition of the techniques of formal realism with the subject matter of fantasy.

As for the texts to be discussed, I have attempted to choose authors representative of a wide range of approaches to the supernatural through the eighteenth and nineteenth centuries. As I said in the preface, however, I did not begin with a body of theory or a set of expectations, but with an interest in these particular stories. Whatever theoretical insights I attempt to apply are used because they throw light on these texts. Chapter 2 discusses the uses of mediated narrative in the romances of Ann Radcliffe (1764–1823), whose characters dramatize the search for a mean between the extremes of atheism and superstition. Besides being an author who cannot well be omitted from an overview of the Gothic novel, Radcliffe provides a baseline for the rest of the study. She also serves as an example of the economical use of strange events to perform two functions: to testify to the allure of the putative supernatural but also to demonstrate that the supernatural (whether real or feigned) presents no danger to a person both rational and devout. In common with her culture, Radcliffe apparently holds that reason and faith are allies rather than foes and that superstitious fear is interdicted by both. At the same time, she shows how the supernatural can safely be "entertained" (in the sense of "giving hospitality to" and "allowing oneself to think about") without firm belief, without danger to a rational world view, and indeed with some benefits. By taming the lure of the supernatural, she shows the universe to be ultimately safe rather than menacing. This impression of safety is enhanced by her editorial pose, which displaces problematic events into a comfortably remote past.

The complicated documentary format of the two Germanic novels treated in chapter 3 conveys a world view that contrasts with Radcliffe's. Both of these authors (at least as revealed in their editorial personae) convey a warning of immediate danger against which they expect the reader to guard himself. *Horrid Mysteries* (1796), in particular, leaves the impression of a universe whose mystery is a threat. The author of *The Necromancer* (1794) is more definitely allied with the prevailing Enlightenment view; Lawrence Flammenberg reveals, rather than the presence of mystery, its absence. Like Radcliffe, he unmasks the pretended supernatural; unlike her, he gives almost no quarter to its attractions. Superstition must be suppressed wherever encountered, and more often than Radcliffe he uses a satirical tone to facilitate this suppression. The universe can be safe, but only if we remain vigilant against the irrational. In *Horrid Mysteries,* on the other hand, Grosse carries both the lure and the threat of the supernatural to extremes, and they remain unreconciled. The narrator holds a conspiracy theory of reality. Whether he stands with or against the greater society depends on how society is defined. At some points he takes his values from mainstream culture, while at other times his primary reference point is the secret organization to which he belongs. This book is preoccupied, as is *The Necromancer* to a lesser degree, with the occult, in the sense of esoteric wisdom.

Next we shall consider the convoluted structure of *Melmoth the Wanderer*, by Irish clergyman Charles Robert Maturin (1780–1824)—author of numerous other Gothic novels and plays—and the novel's resemblances to its near-contemporary *Frankenstein*, by Mary Shelley (1797–1851). The shared motif of the outcast wanderer induced me to pair these novels, and I soon discovered other similarities. One might question the propriety of including *Frankenstein* in a study of the supernatural in fiction. But it is as preoccupied as the German novels with the rational and ethical status of hidden wisdom. The incommunicable secret found in *The Mysteries of Udolpho* and *Horrid Mysteries* is repeated in a different key in Shelley's romance (as well as Maturin's). Though anticipating what would later be called science fiction, *Frankenstein* has the tone and atmosphere of a Gothic novel. Its 1817 preface emphasizes the impossibility of the story's action and explicitly links the tale with superstitious terrors. The creation of the monster, though not supernatural, is preternatural in the sense of going beyond and violating nature as conventionally understood. One question engendered by a scientific world view, of course, is whether there exists any absolute nature whose violation would be evil. The author keeps herself invisible and gives the reader no guidance in answering the questions raised by the text. The reader's role is represented by the addressee of the letter written by Walton, the primary narrator, and we are not allowed to see the answer (if any) to that letter. Maturin is visible in *Melmoth* as editor, and he takes a stance of orthodox Christianity. The text's multiple witnesses of uncertain reliability, however, undercut the editor's simple judgments, so that we cannot be sure whether the response he prescribes is adequate. Maturin's narrators are more numerous and temporal displacement more extreme than in *Frankenstein*.

Chapter 5 moves into the midnineteenth century to explore *A Srange Story*, by Edward Bulwer-Lytton (1803–73), and three tales by Joseph Sheridan Le Fanu (1814–73), all linked by the "occult doctor" motif. Like *Frankenstein* and unlike *Melmoth*, these authors set their stories' action in a time closer to the reader's own, and they address a matter of immediate concern to their own era—the relationship between science and the supernatural realm. While both use mediated narrative, they provide a fruitful contrast between an obtrusive, didactic author (Lytton as editor) and one who remains invisible (Le Fanu). These differences correspond to a contrast between an ultimately benign universe and a hostile or incomprehensible one. Though he calls attention to the unreliability of witnesses, Lytton makes his own position clear through introduction and footnotes, as well as arranging the narrator's experiences to support that position. Lytton stands against the scientific materialism of his culture and for faith in a spiritual realm whose truth overarches and includes scientific truth. In Le Fanu's stories, on the other hand, science seems to reveal a universe whose bleakness is unrelieved by any demonstrable reality beyond the material. Truth is inaccessible. The figure presented as the voice of authoritative knowledge—Dr. Hesselius—proves to be inadequate, and the author offers no overt guidance. Unlike Lytton, he prescribes no philosophic response for the reader.

The narrative structure of Bram Stoker's *Dracula* also renders its author invisible. In this novel we discover a subtle instance of the way documents can paradoxically both verify (by conveying the impression of firsthand, temporally immediate evidence) and cast doubt upon (by reminding us that each bit of testimony is limited by the subjective perception of the witness, with no omniscient narrator to validate its authority) the "facts" of ostensibly supernatural experience. Though Stoker (1847–1912) does not speak in his own person, the overall tenor of the book suggests that he, like Lytton, opposes the prevailing scientific materialism of his time. Stoker displays the scientific world view at first in conflict with the supernatural one and later in service to it. Like Le Fanu, however, he leaves the ultimate evaluation much more in the reader's hands than does Lytton.

Each of the texts, in its own way, invites the reader's judgment upon, identification with, or dissociation from the characters' attitudes toward the supernatural in both the higher and lower senses. And the mode in which the invitation is presented must reveal, however obliquely, the implied author's slant upon these themes. Wayne Booth suggests that no author achieves (though he may assume a pose of) absolute detachment from his subject matter, nor is it morally responsible to do so: "Even the novel in which no narrator is dramatized creates an implicit picture of an author who stands behind the scenes." No matter how much he tries to efface himself, "the author cannot choose to avoid rhetoric; he can choose only the kind of rhetoric he will employ" (Booth, 151, 149). In the texts we will consider, the interaction whereby the reader fills the gaps deliberately left open for him by the author produces a collaborative evaluation of the characters' world view. If supernatural fantasy in general has any characteristic "alethetic" function (in Koelb's terms), this, I believe, is it.

2

The Fantastic-Uncanny in the Novels of Ann Radcliffe

Readers familiar with the romances of Mrs. Radcliffe will recognize that she does not practice the pure fantastic. All her novels resolve themselves into tales of the uncanny, except for *Gaston de Blondeville,* which features a "real" ghost. In none of her books does the validity of the supernatural phenomena remain in question. Rather, she takes pains to assure us (with the single exception) that all the characters' eerie experiences can be explained naturally. As the plot unfolds, however, characters seriously entertain the idea of the supernatural, suspect the presence of ghosts, and debate the reality of the spiritual world. Radcliffe's earlier novels thus fall into the category of the fantastic-uncanny and *Gaston de Blondeville* into the fantastic-marvelous. I intend to examine the techniques that sustain the atmosphere of the fantastic for most of the duration of the narrative. We shall find in Radcliffe's novels a concern with the reliability of sense perception, the testimony of witnesses, temporal displacement, and the relationship among and distance between narrator, editor, commentator, and reader. Through these concerns we shall discover what functions the supernatural performs in her work and how the fantastic mode facilitates these functions.

Why does Radcliffe use the imagined supernatural at all, if at last it is only to be explained away? Before addressing that question, we must briefly consider one function that ghost stories served for the seventeenth- and eighteenth-century mind (and thus may serve in the experience of Radcliffean heroes and heroines). At this period reports of apparitions and portents were often published as factual (for example, by Defoe and Fielding, as discussed below). The expressed purpose of such accounts is not to arouse a frisson of terror, but to instruct. A visitation from beyond death proves the existence of the soul and, therefore, in many apologetic writings of the time, contributes to proving the existence of God Himself. Cataloguing supernatural phenomena strikes a blow against materialism. Not only spirits appearing by divine permission for a good purpose are thus used (exemplified in fiction by the

Otranto ghost); so are instances of the diabolical supernatural. And while the aphorism, "Fair needs foul," with its dualistic implications, may not be orthodox, the notion that God cannot exist without His Adversary is frequently encountered. Since God and Satan are thought to imply each other logically, reports of the latter's depredations strengthen belief in the former. Conversely, as Keith Thomas puts it, "When the Devil was banished to Hell, God himself was confined to working through natural causes" (Thomas, *Religion and the Decline of Magic,* 639). As everyone knows, Cotton Mather's *Wonders of the Invisible World* (1693), like the Salem witchcraft trials, made its appearance *after* secular rationalism began to undermine belief in that world. Joseph Glanvill's *Saducismus Triumphatus* (1681) contains, not theological arguments, but cases of witchcraft and apparitions. ("Sadducee," originally referring to the New Testament party that disbelieved in life after death—an appropriate name for those skeptical of ghosts—is used in this period to mean simply "atheist.") Though these instances antedate Radcliffe by a hundred years, the connection between religion and the dark supernatural can be traced into the eighteenth century.

R. D. Stock, charting attitudes toward the numinous through the Restoration and eighteenth century, explores the way belief in witchcraft bolstered belief in God. Stock says that those who credited the contemporary action of the Devil "wished to affirm an enchanted world in opposition to the world of dead mechanism, the world of mere extension and movement, ushered in by the new philosophy" (Stock, *The Holy and the Daemonic from Sir Thomas Browne to William Blake,* 65). In addition to Glanvill he cites other seventeenth-century treatises such as Henry More's *Antidote against Atheisme* (1653) and Meric Casaubon's *Treatise Proving Spirits, Witches, and Supernatural Operations, by Pregnant Instances and Evidences* (1672). The witchcraft controversy faded in the eighteenth century, to be replaced by debates on the occurrence of miracles in the modern world. Most Englishmen of the day believed that the age of miracles had ended with the New Testament era. The attempt to rationalize away "the non-rational or supranatural side of religious experience"—the numinous or demonic—illustrates how the proponents of the new philosophy distrusted this aspect of religion as "superstition and fanaticism" (Stock, 3). Hume, we recall, asserts that the more exceptional the event in question, the stronger the evidence needed to support it; miracles, being the most extraordinary of events, required a degree of proof scarcely attainable. Among Christian theorists, one facet of the rationalizing tendency was a continuing debate about the eternity of Hell, in which attempts were made to prove damnation a temporary state and remove retributive justice from religion (see D. P. Walker). On the other hand, throughout the period many "inventive and influential writers ... resisted the rationalizing of religion" (Stock, 260). Among them is Daniel Defoe, with his numinous epiphanies and particular providences in *Robinson Crusoe*. Even Samuel Richardson at midcentury and the Gothic writers at its close explore "*spiritual horror* in the novel" (Stock, 262, his emphasis). Stock holds with Rudolf Otto that "the desire for the numinous, when unappeased by authentic religion, will seek satisfaction in such alternatives as the ghost story" (Stock, 115–16).

This quest, of course, renders the seeker liable to the dangers of superstition. The challenge facing Radcliffe's heroes and heroines is to find a way of eschewing materialism while also shunning the hazardous vice of superstition. A pair of interlocutors in Hume's *Dialogues Concerning Natural Religion* (1779, but written in the fifties) encapsulates two opposing attitudes toward such credulity. Philo, the radical skeptic, takes a purist stance: "But in proportion to my veneration for true religion is my abhorrence of vulgar superstitions." Cleanthes counters, "Religion, however corrupted, is still better than no religion at all." The latter advocates maintaining "the doctrine of a future state" at all costs (Hume, 87). Though this interchange refers primarily to religious "superstition," as supposedly epitomized by Roman Catholic practices, for eighteenth-century Englishmen the transition between such superstition and the ghostly kind was an easy and natural one, as illustrated by innumerable Gothic romances centered upon the presumed terrors and abominations of conventual life. Novelists who explain away their own apparitions manage to steer between these two poles. As Geoffrey Hartman says of Milton and the later poets who adopted his mode of dealing with supernatural figures, these novelists exemplify "a new power of self-determination vis-à-vis the spiritual environment in which we live and move and have our being" (Hartman, "False Themes and Gentle Minds," 287). In such writers the poetic imagination plays the role of an enchanter who is not possessed by spirits but rather is able to invoke and dismiss them at will. Free of any fear (or hope) that the old superstitions may genuinely revive, novelists like Radcliffe can flirt with supernatural manifestations yet finally repudiate them. Radcliffe's heroines benefit from the sublime overtones of these manifestations but emerge untainted by superstition. In Hartman's words, the Gothic novelists "toyed with forbidden fire . . . and called up the ghosts they wished to subdue" (Hartman, 284).

Earlier in the century (for example, in the writings of Defoe) supernatural phenomena under providential direction tend to intervene aggressively in characters' lives. J. Paul Hunter (in *The Reluctant Pilgrim*), among others, takes note of Defoe's use of special providences in *Robinson Crusoe* (1719). In this novel, probably partly modeled on real-life spiritual autobiographies, Crusoe interprets dreams, odd coincidences, and other natural but striking events, such as deliverances from danger so extraordinary as to appear quasi-miraculous, as direct signs from God. The action of *Robinson Crusoe* thus answers affirmatively the question of particular providences: "Does God directly intervene in the lives of individuals?" Leo Braudy suggests that the novel's "preoccupation with Providence may have been the expression of an actual providential anxiety, a desperate need to assert that God had not left the world behind, even though the orders of society and culture seemed to possess none of their old authority or effectiveness" (Braudy, *Narrative Form in History and Fiction,* 85). If so, this preoccupation is a further instance of the way intense interest in such issues as special providences grew up at a time when the existence and operations of the supernatural had ceased to be a matter of universal consensus.

Besides such phenomena as coincidences and extraordinary deliverances, whose intepretation as quasi-supernatural depends on the subject's faith, actual visions and apparitions could be presented as evidence of God's existence and care. Thomas notes that "as atheism became a greater threat to true religion than Popery," eighteenth-century Protestant theologians "became more sympathetic to the idea of ghosts" (Thomas, 591). Defoe's purportedly factual ghost story, *A True Relation of the Apparition of One Mrs. Veal* (1706), portrays a revenant whose visit is divinely sanctioned. Mrs. Veal's appearance demonstrates the possibility of communication between the spiritual and mortal worlds, but more important is the Christian consolation the ghost brings to her surviving friend. This apparition then, though more blatantly supernatural, constitutes a special providence just as do Crusoe's experiences. *A True Relation* prefigures ghosts such as the one in *Otranto* (1764), sent back into the world to execute justice upon evil and reward virtue. Terrible only to the wicked, to the virtuous such a spirit serves to demonstrate the immortality of the soul and the existence and nature of God.

A similar connection between apparitions and Providence is made by Fielding's "Examples of the Interposition of Providence in the Detection and Punishment of Murder" (1752). What providential coincidences do, in fiction, for Crusoe, purportedly factual apparitions (less tranquil than that of Mrs. Veal) do for the readers of these "Examples." They demonstrate divine intervention in the course of mundane events. The cases catalogued in Fielding's work resemble synopses of detective novels, with motive, material evidence, clues, and the unraveling of mystery. The new philosophy's concern with testimony and proof is a prominent feature of these case histories. While some devices for uncovering the truth are purely circumstantial or psychological, many involve the ghost of the victim or other supernatural phenomena such as blood dripping from a severed hand, blood obscuring the words in a book, or a paper denouncing the murderers that appears out of nowhere. All these events are assigned to God's direct action. Fielding attributes a recent increase in the number of murders, and therefore in occasions for supernatural vengeance, to "that general neglect (I wish I could not say contempt) of religion, which hath within these few years so fatally overspread this whole nation" (Fielding, "Examples," 3: 146). Fielding asserts that some of the apparitions reported "have been so well and faithfully attested, that to reject them with a hasty disbelief, seems to argue more of an obstinate and stubborn infidelity, than of a sound and sober reason" (Fielding, "Examples," 3: 116). He thus recognizes the likelihood of his readers' doubting the verity of ghost stories and consequently needs to defend the reports against skepticism (an analogy to the writer of ghost stories who postulates the reader's initial disbelief in ghosts). Belief in the supernatural (whether "higher" or "lower") cannot be taken for granted. We also note that he links faith in God to belief in ghosts.

In *Tom Jones* (1749), Fielding makes a somewhat ironic connection between the two. In this episode a soldier imagines he has seen the fiery ghost of a recently deceased comrade. His story, though believed by "the women present," wins no credit from his superiors, especially the officer, who "though a very religious man, was free from all terrors of this kind" (*Tom Jones,* bk. VII, chap. 14, 326). The qualifying phrase "though... religious" seems to imply that superstitious fear customarily accompanies religious faith. In this context superstition apparently degrades religion, rather than religion lending respectability to belief in ghosts. A similar implication arises from Partridge's farcical ghost story in which the squire who doubts the "spirit" is labeled an "atheist" (*Tom Jones,* bk. VIII, chap. 11, 387). The credulous Partridge, however, is hardly to be thought a reliable spokesman for Fielding. The famous episode of the play, when Partridge trembles in fear of the ghost in *Hamlet,* further holds superstition up to mockery (*Tom Jones,* bk. XVI, chap. 5). Apparently Fielding's sober beliefs, presumably expressed in "Examples of the Interposition of Providence," do not include condoning the use of ghostly terror for entertainment.

"Examples of the Interposition of Providence" precedes *The Castle of Otranto* by only twelve years. Walpole's novel offers a fictional illustration of Fielding's theme of just retribution through supernatural agency. Walpole's first explicit imitator, Clara Reeve, adopts his central plot motif of a spirit who appears with divine sanction to reveal hidden guilt (*The Old English Baron,* 1777). In chapter 31 of *Rasselas* (1759), Samuel Johnson has Imlac assert belief in the power of the dead to return, citing the universality of this belief as evidence for its truth. Imlac also maintains that if ghosts do appear, they have no power or wish to harm the innocent. Though Boswell does not commit himself on the subject of Johnson's belief in ghosts, Johnson seems to have remained open to the possibility of their existence. He is quoted as declaring, in 1778, that the reality of ghosts is "a question, whether in theology or philosophy, one of the most important that can come before the human understanding" (Boswell, 951). As late as 1784, he says of a spectral vision purportedly seen by Thomas, Lord Lyttleton, "I am so glad to have every evidence of the spiritual world, that I am willing to believe it" (Boswell, 1296). Although Johnson's remarks illustrate a continuing awareness, among at least some thinkers, of the potential theological significance of apparitions, contemporary critics do not seem to have found any such significance in fictional apparitions. Richard Hurd, in "Letters on Chivalry and Romance" (1762), addresses only the aesthetic, not the moral and theological, issues involved in evoking supernatural terror. According to Hurd, stories that employ the machinery of "superstition" are directed primarily to the skeptic: "We must distinguish between the *popular belief* and *that of the reader.* The fictions of poetry do, in some degree at least, require the *first* . . . but when the poet has this advantage on his side . . . he dispenses with the *last,* and gives his reader leave to be as sceptical, and as incredulous, as he pleases" (Hurd, 322). Hurd clearly expects distance between the world views of readers and fictional characters. Aesthetic treatment of ghosts becomes popular after the culture's consensus about their existence and significance has broken down. While a romance hero or heroine's life may be changed by a visit from the spectral realm, the romance reader has permission to remain "sceptical" and "incredulous," drawing as much, or as little, spiritual benefit from the apparition as he pleases.

Radcliffe has the characters in her early work, *A Sicilian Romance* (1790), debate the reality and theological import of hauntings. (By "Radcliffe," I mean, of course, the implied-author-within-the-text.) The heroine's governess, discussing the possible existence of ghosts, says, "Who shall say that anything is impossible to God? We know that he has made us, who are embodied spirits; he, therefore, can make unembodied spirits" (*Sicilian Romance,* 1: 83). Much like Imlac, the same speaker further asserts, "Such spirits, if indeed they have ever been seen, can have appeared only by the express permission of God, and for some very singular purposes" (*Sicilian Romance,* 1: 84). Here the existence of ghosts is made contingent on that of God. If the former cannot exist without the latter, then the true apparition of a ghost constitutes a strong argument for the reality of the Divine. Radcliffe is far from denying the reality of the spiritual realm, yet avoids lending support to credulous superstition unworthy of an enlightened age. Her novels maintain a balance between these two attitudes by keeping their apparitions suspended in the realm of the fantastic until the end of the story. This conversation from *A Sicilian Romance* is a good example of Radcliffe's calling up ghosts in order to subdue them. In her world we can entertain belief in the supernatural in general but disbelieve every particular supernatural event. Radcliffe's "suggestive obscurity" allows us to "feel the full impression of the world of shadows although she stops short of anything really supernatural" (Varma, 104, 107). In other words, she gives us the awareness of a reality beyond the material without demanding a positive act of belief from us; we have our Enlightenment cake and eat it with Gothic icing. In Joel Porte's words, she demonstrates that "the proper business of the orthodox novel of terror" is "to expand the soul religiously" (Porte, "In the Hands of an Angry God," 43).

A dissertation by John Roger Peavoy shares my interest in the religious aspect of Gothic fiction but approaches analysis of the supernatural in this fiction differently. To begin with, he sets different boundaries for the field, with the statement, "The supernatural is the defining element in Gothic fiction" (Peavoy, 1). I, instead, take the subgenre's defining elements to be the typical setting and the typical villain or villain-hero. Some works generally considered Gothic have no hint of the supernatural, such as du Maurier's *Rebecca.* And Peavoy's definition entails classifying every ghost story as Gothic, an invitation to a Humpty-Dumpty distortion of usage. This definition, though, is only a prelude to his thesis, which involves dividing the functions of the supernatural in Gothic fiction into three categories: (a) The supernatural agent is benign, serving the ends of Providence by avenging a wrong. *Otranto* is the textbook example of this category. (b) The "supernatural" phenomena are explained away. Radcliffe, of course, provides the material for this category. Peavoy concludes that "the effect of her technique is to divorce a character from his experience," because the heroine, throughout her ordeal, remains innocent and untouched by evil (Peavoy, 12). The illusory nature of the haunting symbolizes this insulation. Like the "enchanter" poets discussed by Hartman in "False Themes and Gentle Minds," enchanters who are "no longer coerced or compelled" (Hartman, 288), Radcliffe summons her ghosts to impart a salutary lesson, then dismisses them without allowing them to taint the protagonist's soul. The Radcliffe heroine finds that "what had appeared to be a sinister and terrifying supernatural world in which the rules of common sense did not apply was actually a temporary aberration in her perception of reality" (Peavoy, 12). (c) In this category the supernatural agents are both real and evil. According to Peavoy, this is the only one of the three kinds of novels in which characters have the opportunity for meaningful choice. Hence books of this type (e.g., *The Monk*) "allow for moral seriousness." He asserts, "Their use of the supernatural does not, of course, ensure quality. But at least it does not prevent it" (Peavoy, 13, 14). Implicit in this argument lies the assumption that the supernatural in fiction usually *does* preclude quality, and only a special defense can justify its use.

I have no quarrel with Peavoy's tripartite scheme (though we shall find an interesting deviation from these categories in *Horrid Mysteries,* wherein the author attempts to explain away the supernatural but still leaves an impression of a "terrifying and sinister" universe). It generates useful analysis of Gothic novels that feature the supernatural. My classification of the texts, however, falls along Todorov's lines, as explained above, and focuses upon the way narrative technique supports or undercuts intimations of the other-worldly. My point of contact with Peavoy concerns the connection between religion and the supernatural in these novels—though he holds that the connection usually works to the novels' disadvantage. My attitude is closer to one expressed by Stock in the statement that Gothic novels "attempt to exercise the imagination in the non-rational areas scorned and perhaps feared by the apostles of the Enlightenment. And if . . . a deep spiritual understanding cannot be attained without an immediate and strong sense of evil, then these books have their place in our religious education" (Peavoy, 313). What the experience of reading a Gothic novel actually contributes to the reader's "religious education" is a moot point. The protagonists, however, often undergo such an education, directed toward purifying and refining their beliefs about the relations between the seen and unseen worlds.

Hartman points out that the main currents of Enlightenment thought strove to unite reason and fiction, to the exclusion of myth and the irrational. But fiction such as Radcliffe's, rather than banishing these dubious elements, shows how they can perform useful functions under reason's rule. Rationality may tame rather than exclude romance. Wordsworth's practice of evoking the feelings associated with the supernatural while dispensing with supernatural entities is, according to Hartman, the ultimate development of this trend. The rowboat episode in the first book of *The Prelude* resembles Radcliffe's terrifying incidents in one point at least, its focus on the response of the protagonist rather than the factual content of the experience. In the Romantic poets' domestication of the supernatural we find a parallel to the Gothic novelists' depiction of romantic subject matter in realistic style. Just as Coleridge (in *Lyrical Ballads)* professedly attempted to render supernatural incidents in a manner true to human nature, Walpole and his successors tried, in the midst of wildly improbable fictional situations, to "conduct the mortal agents . . . according to the rules of probability; in short, to make them think, speak, and act, as it might be supposed mere men and women would do" (Walpole, 7–8). This strategy, to achieve the desired "willing suspension of disbelief," requires an attention to realistic particularity of detail as stringent as Richardson's or Fielding's. The contrast between romantic subject and realistic technique parallels the contrast between two attitudes toward that subject matter—the characters' tendency toward acceptance of the supernatural and the reader's presumed skepticism. The implied reader, like the implied author, stands on the less credulous side of the line and therefore can benefit from the author's enchanter-like manipulation of the supernatural without taking the characters' risk of being entrapped by superstition.

"Expanding the soul religiously" is only one use Radcliffe makes of the apparent supernatural. At the other extreme, she uses strange events to display the deleterious effects of superstition. A third use of supernatural phenomena stands apart from the other two in its playfulness, an indulgence in other-worldly speculation for sheer pleasure, with no immediate moral application. The religious function of strange events, as we have seen, is made explicit in *A Sicilian Romance.* The ghost in this novel is actually the wife of a wicked marquis, the heroine's mother, supposed dead but really imprisoned by her husband. While the cause of the haunting of the castle's abandoned wing remains in doubt, though, the possibility of ghosts occupies the minds of the characters. The governess mentioned above in *A Sicilian Romance,* represented as an accomplished, educated gentlewoman, keeps an open mind on the question: "I do not say that spirits *have* appeared; but if several discreet unprejudiced persons were to assure me that they had seen one, I should not be proud or bold enough to reply—'it is impossible'" (*Sicilian Romance,* 1: 83–84). Though ostensibly a product of a Gothic era, she speaks like a judicious Enlightenment philosopher (such as Hume writing on miracles) weighing the credibility of the witnesses reporting an extraordinary event. She seems to fill the role of *raisonneuse,* reminding us as well as the heroine that belief in the spiritual world is not beneath the attention of an intelligent person. (Her distance from the narrator and implied author—in Booth's phrase—seems to be less than that of the other characters.) And she emphatically links this belief to the awareness that "nothing is impossible to God." In this novel the hints of ghostly terrors are partly intended to direct our thoughts to mysteries beyond "the limited powers of our minds" (*A Sicilian Romance,* 1: 83).

When acceptance of the supernatural engenders fear rather than faith (as is usually the case in Radcliffe when a ghost is directly encountered), it is called superstition and condemned. A paradigmatic instance appears in *Mysteries of Udolpho,* when a spectral voice interrupts the deliberations of Montoni and his confederates (*Udolpho,* vol. 2, chap. 7). The villains attempt to cover their fear with jeering bravado; even Montoni, who elsewhere expresses contempt for superstitious terror, is "visibly and greatly disordered" (*Udolpho,* 291). Later DuPont, one of the heroes, recounts how he produced the mysterious voice by concealing himself in a secret passage. His motive was to "awaken the consciences" of the villains, for "the most impious men are often the most superstitious" (*Udolpho,* 460). His well-meant deception inspires no repentance, but only "a general alarm among Montoni's people," which the heroine Emily considers herself "weak" for sharing (*Udolpho,* 460). We observe that the moral effect of a quasi-supernatural experience depends on the character of the patient. While the maid Annette, with her love of wonders, finds in the castle of Udolpho only a series of fleeting emotional extravagances, Emily mines her isolation and fear for uplifting meditations, and Montoni's henchmen react to spectral phenomena by becoming more confirmed in their villainy. Thus, though DuPont's remark about "impious men" implies an inverse relation between religious faith and belief in ghosts, this assumption must be qualified by consideration of the actors and circumstances in each particular case. Emily chastises herself for partaking of the superstitious weakness of criminals, but she feels no self-reproach about contemplating the possible nearness of her father's spirit, a possibility that inspires her to a "fortitude" that "endeavours to practise the precepts" inculcated by her late parents (*Udolpho*, 92).

Nor does the purely aesthetic indulgence of supernatural fancy receive unqualified condemnation. Indeed, in *Udolpho* this kind of play seems to constitute harmless refreshment. Emily's father, represented as a paragon of philosophic virtue, admits to indulging "fairy visions and romantic images," which he associates with "that high enthusiasm, which wakes the poet's dream" (*Udolpho*, 15). In the woods at evening Emily fancies that she hears "the voice of the spirit of the woods" (*Udolpho*, 15). The lower classes, too, sometimes contemplate supernatural entities from a sportive distance instead of involving themselves in the terrors of superstitious credulity. When Emily wonders at a Tuscan village's invocation to a sea-nymph, accompanied by floral offerings, she is told that "nobody *believes* in such things, but our old songs tell of them" (*Udolpho*, 421). Again an association is made between entertainment of the supernatural without belief and the powers of poetry. Emily's father draws an explicit parallel between poetic fancy and supernatural power when he tells her, "If she [fancy] has given you one of her spells, you need not envy those of the fairies" (*Udolpho*, 16). These spells remain, of course, purely a temporary refreshment; his stern admonitions about the hazards of sensibility indicate that he would not allow such fancies to influence the serious business of life. Composing her verses on glowworms and fairies, Emily resembles Hartman's poets who control their spirits so thoroughly that "the haunted ground of Romance is aestheticized; the gods become diminutive, picturesque, charming" (Hartman, 289). While apparently productive of no great spiritual growth, this playful manipulation of the supernatural does produce an aesthetic distance that, if maintained, would preclude superstitious fear. This use of the supernatural is not prominent in Radcliffe's novels, but its presence is nonetheless significant.

Radcliffe's narrative structure can perform simultaneously the tasks of both highlighting the spiritual implications of the action and distancing the reader from the characters' beliefs. *A Sicilian Romance*, like several of her other novels, prepares us for a tale of the imagined supernatural by a narrative frame. The first-person narrator of this frame represents herself as a traveler who notices the ruins of Mazzini Castle and falls into conversation with a friar walking there. He gives her access to a manuscript written by a descendant of the Mazzinis featured in the story. From this document the narrator takes an abstract, later rearranging the incidents in her own words. The tale is thus distanced from the reader by several removes. For Elizabeth MacAndrew the purpose of this kind of mediated narrative, so characteristic of Gothic fiction, is to create "a structure that makes a closed-off region within an outer world" (MacAndrew, 109). When the reader is asked to imagine himself "reading a manuscript of shadowy authorship unearthed and presented to him by an unidentified 'editor,' a sense is imparted that he is about to delve into a world that will be difficult to understand." The purpose of the frame story and the tale-within-a-tale is always "to make the world of the novel strange" (MacAndrew, 10, 111). MacAndrew assigns this distance and strangeness the function of alerting the reader to the nature of the genre confronted and its requirement for quasi-symbolic interpretation. As remarked in the previous chapter, the Gothic world is to her a world of the mind. For my purposes, this other, strange realm is one in which the supernatural becomes credible. Wayne Booth lists several modes in which the narrator "may be more or less distant from the *characters* in the story he tells. He may differ morally, intellectually, and temporally" (Booth, 157). Radcliffe makes an emphatic point of the temporal distance between her narrator and her characters. This temporal distance implies intellectual distance, for the intervening centuries have wrought changes in beliefs about the nature of reality. In reading these stories we partake of a double vision, the vision of the characters and that of the implied author. Some characters, but usually not the protagonist, view the mundane world as "enchanted ground," where marvels may be suspected of lurking in every corner. The implied author, however, belongs to a world where a clear separation exists between natural and supernatural, and the invasion of the former by the latter is an occasion for uncertainty and requires supporting evidence to elicit a rational person's assent. The displacing of events into a remote time and place is one way of placating the discursive intellect. (Walpole in *Otranto* works similarly. His preface establishes a condescending distance, while the body of the book indulges the thrill of superstition.) Once the frame of *A Sicilian Romance* has done its preparatory work, the reader is allowed to forget about it until the final page. The frame narrator returns only to point the moral—whether her own, or that of the Mazzini heir writing for a monastic audience, is unclear—that "those who do only THAT WHICH IS RIGHT, endure nothing in misfortune but a trial of their virtue, and from trials well endured, derive the surest claim to the protection of heaven" (*Sicilian Romance,* 2: 216). This concluding statement recalls the friar's remark in the opening pages referring to the ruin of the castle as "a singular instance of the retribution of Heaven" (*Sicilian Romance,* 1: 3). In fact the author never tells us how the castle fell into ruin, but the remark nevertheless alerts us to the connection between supernatural visitations and Divine Providence. Though this novel contains no explicit, proven supernatural events, it has affinities with Peavoy's reading of *Otranto* as shaped by a "providential plan...every move of which has been predetermined by a supernatural power [i.e., God]" (Peavoy, 12, 34). The narrative situation in *A Sicilian Romance* is more complicated than that in *Otranto,* because the dramatized first-person narrator of Radcliffe's frame is not the only commentator on the supposed medieval chronicle. In *Otranto* (as originally published, with Walpole's authorship cloaked under a fiction of editorship) we have to deal with only two levels of commentary on the tale, the editor's and the chronicler's. In *A Sicilian Romance* the friar who offers the manuscript to the Radcliffe persona provides a third perspective on the action. Though temporally he inhabits the same world as the frame narrator, his comment on "the retribution of Heaven" shows that culturally he stands closer to the original author of the tale. He therefore mediates between the enlightened present and the superstitious past. *Otranto,* on the other hand, offers only a marked contrast between the credulity of the narrative and the patronizing skepticism of the frame (praising the chronicler's technique but emphatically dissociating itself from his beliefs).

Radcliffe's best-known novel, *The Mysteries of Udolpho* (1794), dispenses with a frame. Its omniscient narrator takes full advantage of her position, beginning the history of the heroine, Emily, with her parents' marriage. But *Udolpho* employs the discourse of the fantastic extensively in dialogue and interpolated narratives. Robert Day refers to the latter, in early fiction of all sorts, as "the digressive and structurally inartistic 'history' which brings the story to a standstill" (Day, *Told in Letters,* 24). In Radcliffe and other Gothic novelists, however, though such "histories" may display no direct relevance to the main plot, they often serve a thematic or mood-setting function. When the interpolated tale *is* connected to the main plot, it often takes the form of a discovered manuscript or an oral recitation that reveals hidden facts the heroine needs to know. Some truth buried in the distant past needs to be brought to light. This situation corresponds to Todorov's paradigm of the "duality" of the detective story: "This novel contains not one but two stories: the story of the crime and the story of the investigation.... The first story, that of the crime, ends before the second begins" (Todorov, *The Poetics of Prose,* 44). A Gothic novel often features the revelation of a crime whose secret overshadows a house (both in the sense of a family and of a dwelling). The second story, the one immediately before us, tells "how the reader (or the narrator)"—but in this case the heroine who is center of consciousness—"has come to know about" the long-buried crime (Todorov, *The Poetics of Prose,* 45). In Gothic fiction the protagonist usually discovers the truth from an old manuscript or an oral confession rather than through investigation of clues. Moreover, he or she falls into personal danger, so that this fiction properly belongs to Todorov's category of suspense rather than pure detective story.

Emily in *The Mysteries of Udolpho* certainly experiences enough personal danger to satisfy most readers' thirst for suspense. At the same time, though, she plays the role of an investigator, not only examining material clues such as the trail of blood leading to the tower where her aunt is imprisoned, but also weighing hearsay reports of eerie and perhaps supernatural events. The history of Udolpho's dark past comes to her through the maid Annette, who in turn has heard the story from servants of longer tenure at the castle. Even Annette, inclined to credit the rumors of Signora Laurentini's ghost, continually punctuates her recital with the refrain that "they say" the lady died in the nearby wood and therefore haunts it (*Udolpho*, 236–39). Purportedly supernatural incidents are most often reported to characters by other characters, not recounted by the narrator or witnessed by Emily herself. For instance, two manservants (and later Annette) tell Emily of an apparition that walks the castle ramparts by night. Emily, whose world view presumably stands closer to the narrator's than do the other characters' views, reacts with skepticism. Further doubt is cast on the reliability of the reports by their source, the lower-class figures used by Radcliffe for quasi-Shakespearean comic relief. Indeed, the superstitious, credulous characters in her fiction are most often servants. The narratee (to employ Gerald Prince's term) is often tacitly invited to join the narrator in patronizing such characters' credulity. The maid Annette, for instance, "dearly loved the marvellous, and had heard of a circumstance, connected with the castle, that highly gratified this taste" (*Udolpho*, 235). The slight hyperbole of "highly gratified" and the cosy colloquialism, "dearly loved," establish the distance between Annette and the narrator-narratee alliance.

When Emily herself experiences dubious phenomena and entertains speculation about the supernatural, the effects are more subtle. Shortly after her father's death, while musing on "the probable state of departed spirits," she is startled by a sound that gives her "a sudden terror of something supernatural" (*Udolpho*, 95). Her psychological vulnerability at this moment is in contrast to her predominant rationality, inculcated by her father's teachings. The vagueness of that something leaves open the possibility that she has imagined or misinterpreted whatever she has heard. On another occasion Emily hears mysterious music and speculates that it may be a message from Heaven, where her father is watching over her. In this passage she thrice uses the word "perhaps" (*Udolpho*, 340). She bases her supernatural interpretation of the music on hearsay—"it has been affirmed," "Father Pierre and Father Antoine declared," and "my dear father himself, once said" that such celestial music is sometimes heard (*Udolpho*, 340). The impersonal passive of "it has been affirmed," in particular, conveys a sense of the dubious. Uncertainty also overshadows her attempts to control the terror that touches her at these moments: "If the spirits of those we love ever return to us [they must surely be benevolent]" (*Udolpho,* 95). But do they? Emily's father, when ill and near death, addresses this question: "I hope we shall be permitted to look down on those we have left on the earth, but I can only hope it. Futurity is much veiled from our eyes, and faith and hope are our only guides concerning it. We are not enjoined to believe, that disembodied spirits watch over the friends they have loved, but we may innocently hope it" (*Udolpho,* 67). Speculations like these prepare us for ghostly visitations before Emily finds herself confronted with hauntings. We may note that Emily's mysterious music is not explained, but left to linger as part of the fantastic atmosphere. The word "veiled" recalls *Udolpho's* famous "black veil" episode, which, says Peavoy, illustrates "the typical condition of a Radcliffe heroine . . . trying unsuccessfully to understand what is happening around her" (*Peavoy,* 85). The "misperception" represented by the veil may be seen as a paradigm of every Gothic protagonist's condition (Peavoy, 84). He or she views the true nature of the universe as hidden by a veil, a metaphor prominent in many Gothic novels. What is veiled may be futurity, evil, the supernatural, or the absence of the supernatural. Ghostly visitations allure because they seem to promise a lifting of the veil.

In *Udolpho* preparation for apparitions is partly effected by ghostly narratives having nothing to do with the mystery of Udolpho itself. Quite early in the novel, soon after the death of Emily's father, she is told of a nearby abandoned chateau, shunned in superstitious dread as haunted. Even when Emily stays at this chateau (newly inhabited by the Count de Villefort) after her escape from Udolpho, its "ghost" has no part in the main action. The apparition serves, instead, to heighten our impression of this world as one in which supernatural events may occur.

The Mysteries of Udolpho does, however, contain one ghost whose status is not (within its own text) reduced to the natural. This figure appears, not in the main narrative, but in an interpolated tale read by the manservant Ludovico. This story, "The Provencal Tale," concerns (like Fielding's Providential interpositions) the punishment of crime. A baron is visited by the spirit of a murdered knight. Thinking the ghost a living man, the baron follows it through a secret passage to a wood where the bloody corpse lies. While the main action of *Udolpho* is assigned to the sixteenth century, the interpolated tale is set in the twelfth. Within the tale, moreover, the baron's experience is set in the distant past, contrasted with "these degenerate days" (*Udolpho,* 552). We could hardly find a clearer example of temporal distancing, as well as of the fact that romance tends to be, in the Bloomian sense, belated. The latecoming poet, says Bloom, "seeks to exorcise the necessary guilt of his ingratitude by turning his precursor into a fouled version of the later poet himself" (Bloom, *The Anxiety of Influence*, 62). "Fouled" is too harsh a word for what romance does to its precursors; say, rather, that a romance makes its predecessor into an *incomplete* version of itself. The belated writer looks into the past for an object of imitation; not finding the proper object, he reproduces what he imagines the past ought to have been like (in our period we notice *Ossian,* among others). However far back toward origins we search, moreover, the ideal is placed still further back. In Arthurian lore, for instance, the earliest literary romances, Chrétien's, make reference to an already established tradition. Similarly, Radcliffe's tale-within-a-tale distinguishes between the heroic past and "these degenerate days." Further intellectual distance is imposed by the omniscient narrator's evaluation (inviting our collusion with her against the credulous Ludovico and the writer of the manuscript), "The reader will perceive, that it is strongly tinctured with the superstition of the times" (*Udolpho,* 552). On the other hand, this superstitious tale of remote times is linked to the novel's present (sixteenth century) by Ludovico's frequent pauses, inspired by terror of the eerie noises infesting the castle at that moment. We are reminded of Poe's counterpoint between the presently unfolding horror and the reading of a medieval romance in "The Fall of the House of Usher." Radcliffe's multiple dispacements, however, produce a distancing effect that alerts us to the delusory nature of the supposed haunting. When Ludovico, passing a vigil in a haunted chamber, fancies a voice corresponding to the spectral voice in his tale, the noise turns out to be nothing but "the distant roaring of the sea in the storm" (*Udolpho,* 556). The supernatural dangers are only a product of imagination. In "Usher," on the other hand, reality is revealed as *more* terrible than the narrator imagines. The strangely apposite sounds accompanying Sir Launcelot Canning's romance—an appositeness that the narrator, unlike Ludovico, strives unsuccessfully to deny—are in fact heralds of a horror unsuspected by him, Madeline's eruption from the tomb.

Superstition is not confined to lower-class characters like Ludovico and Annette, but when educated persons fall prey to it, they usually feel shame. Emily often refers to her lapses into superstitious dread as weakness (*Udolpho,* 103 and passim). On one such occasion the narrator says, "It was lamentable that her excellent understanding should have yielded, even for a moment, to the reveries of superstition, or rather to those starts of imagination, which deceive the senses into what can be called nothing less than momentary madness" (*Udolpho,* 102). For Emily these aberrations are only momentary and result from special circumstances, such as her "solitary life," the "infirm state of her nerves," and the recent death of her father (*Udolpho,* 102). These circumstances are required to explain why an "excellent understanding" (united with virtue and piety) would succumb to the "madness" of which (as Foucault says) this era was so much afraid. If her lapses were more than momentary, she would cease to be a safe model for the female reader. That superstitious fear is a form of madness is emphasized by its frequently being contrasted to reason. When recovering from the horror of Montoni's threats, Emily finds that "the astonishment and terrors of superstition, which had, for a moment, so strongly assailed her, now yielded to those of reason" (*Udolpho*, 395). (It is an interesting syntactic elision that results in this sentence's revealing the terrors of reason!) On another occasion it is said of the servants in the haunted chateau that "fear had rendered their minds inaccessible to reason" (*Udolpho*, 543). Rationality and piety together guard against being thrown into terror by "supernatural" suggestions but do not forbid the openness to the other-worldly exhibited by the governess in *Sicilian Romance* and Emily's father in *Udolpho*.

"Suggestive," the single word most often used to characterize Radcliffe's technique, applies particularly well to *The Italian* (1797), whose "suggestiveness" is more smoothly integrated into the main action than *Udolpho*'s. The function of the romance's pervasive atmosphere of supernatural forces, lurking behind the facade of natural malice and intrigue, seems to be articulated by the villain Schedoni. In his dying confession, strangely enough, he appears to act as the author's spokesman:

> The opinions you avowed were rational... but the ardour of your imagination was apparent, and what ardent imagination ever was contented to trust to plain reasoning, or to the evidence of the senses? It may not willingly confine itself to the dull truths of this earth, but, eager to expand its faculties, to fill its capacity, and to experience its own peculiar delights, soars after new wonders into a world of its own! (*The Italian*, 4: 192)

Schedoni terms this "ardour" a weakness that renders Vivaldi (the hero) "especially liable to superstition" (*The Italian*, 4: 191). In view of Schedoni's villainy, we may have reason to regard his opinions on the weakness of belief in the supernatural as the opposite of the author's. On the other hand, Vivaldi acknowledges the justness of the rebuke and realizes that for him "conjecture had never assumed the stability of opinion" on the subject of ghosts (*The Italian*, 4: 192). Conjecture is as far as the novel goes toward acceptance of the supernatural, without settling the question of how reasonable such conjecture may be.

Both Peavoy and Stock read the scene just cited as a clear condemnation of Vivaldi's preoccupation with the supernatural. Stock goes so far as to assert that superstitious dread is always condemned in *The Italian*, even when its immediate effect is good (e.g., momentarily awakening the Marchesa's conscience). To these two critics, Schedoni indeed speaks for Radcliffe. And we cannot deny that in the final analysis a chastened Vivaldi does discover his fearful fascination with supernatural experience to be a weakness. But is the final analysis all that counts? Critics such as Stanley Fish (see "Literature in the Reader: Affective Stylistics") would reply in the negative. His interpretive method insists upon the temporal dimension as an essential component. We as readers do not grasp a text as a static whole, but as an unfolding experience. The earlier parts of a syntactic unit (whether sentence, paragraph, or whole poem or novel) arouse expectations that may or may not be fulfilled in the later parts, but the experience—all of it—*is* the meaning. In *The Italian* our experience of sharing Vivaldi's terror and fascination is not cancelled by the later experience of sharing his disillusionment. The earlier response, then, can plausibly be accepted as a part of the intention. Thus the implied author testifies to the allure of the supernatural without giving intellectual assent to it.

By witholding this assent and showing Vivaldi rebuked for lack of stability, *The Italian* avoids the hazard of encouraging superstition. In Radcliffe's novels the distancing techniques and the nonsupernatural denouements reassert, after a temporary plunge into a world of ghostly terrors, the essential rationality of the universe. As Peavoy points out, in this fictional universe, although recognition of spiritual power in the world is a sign of one's goodness, *fear* of the supernatural "is a weakness which leaves one vulnerable" (Peavoy, 77). To be open to the possibility of supernatural intervention in earthly affairs, like the governess in *A Sicilian Romance,* is apparently a component of spiritual health, but, conversely, "the most impious men are often the most superstitious" (*Udolpho,* 460). Unlike Emily and Ellena, finding sublime consolations in the midst of terrifying captivity, impious men labor under an inaccurate view of the nature of reality. Instead of "having their cake and eating it," the victims of superstition suffer the ill effects of the supernatural world view without enjoying its benefits. Protection from the terrors potentially lurking in unexplained phenomena is attained by recognizing that "spirits, if indeed they have ever been seen, can have appeared only by the express permission of God" (*Sicilian Romance,* 84) and thus pose no threat to people of virtue and good judgment.

The Italian contains fewer doubtful phenomena than does *Udolpho,* most of the terrors in the former being generated by the sinister power of the Inquisition. Hovering between solemn fear and uneasy jest, Vivaldi suspects that the elusive monk who persists in following him and his servant Paulo (vol. 1) is a specter. Neither Vivaldi or Paulo has a monopoly on credulity; each in turn urges the other to take a rational view of their pursuer. At the moment when Vivaldi most earnestly entertains the idea of a ghost, he is still far from certainty:

> If this being had *appeared only,* said he to himself, I should, perhaps, have thought it the perturbed spirit of him, who doubtless has been murdered here, and that it led me to discover the deed, that his bones might be removed to holy ground.... If he had either hinted of himself, or had been wholly silent, his appearance and his manner of eluding pursuit are so extraordinary, that I should have yielded, for once, perhaps, to the tales of our grandfathers, and thought he was the spectre of a murdered person. (*The Italian,* 1:206)

The conditional clauses, along with the repetition of the words "perhaps" and "thought," embody the tentative nature of the hero's yielding to superstition. The state of mind he attains is, at best, not a firm belief, but only a suspension between belief and doubt.

How far are we meant to share this uncertainty? In volume 1, chapter 6, Vivaldi is awed by the "solemn event" connected with the mysterious monk's advent (*The Italian,* 1: 152). The narrator cites sufficient cause for this awe but implies that Vivaldi's reaction takes him beyond the bounds of a reasonable response:

> His understanding was sufficiently clear and strong to teach him to detect many errors of opinion, that prevailed around him, as well as to despise the common superstitions of his country, and, in the usual state of his mind, he probably would not have paused for a moment on the subject before him; but his passions were now interested, and his fancy awakened.... [H]e would, perhaps, have been somewhat disappointed, to have descended suddenly from the region of fearful sublimity to which he had soared ... to the earth, on which he daily walked. (*The Italian,* 1: 152–53)

Here the narrator invites us to acquiesce in his condescending survey of Vivaldi's wishful thinking. The distance between narrator and narratee decreases as the distance between both and the hero increases. (Though himself ostensibly a countryman of Vivaldi, the narrator speaks like the implied reader, a rational Englishman such as the central character of the introductory frame.) The narratee is admitted to a superior position of recognizing motives of which Vivaldi himself is "unconscious" (*The Italian,* 1: 153). In a subsequent mysterious encounter the gap between hero and narratee closes (vol. 1, chap. 7). When told that Vivaldi's "mood was grave, even to solemnity, and he yielded, though reluctantly, to the awe, which at intervals, returned upon him with the force of a magical spell" (*The Italian,* 1: 188), we receive no hint of scorn for his mood. That he yields only "reluctantly" suggests an atmosphere whose influence it is no disgrace to be unable to resist. And this narrator clearly does not consider awe a despicable emotion; Ellena's laudable sensibility is demonstrated by the awe that accompanies her "dreadful pleasure" in viewing a torrential river, even in the midst of desperate trouble (*The Italian,* 1: 167). Nor can Vivaldi be considered contemptible for pursuing sublimity, when Ellena is commended for displaying the same response to the grandeur of mountain scenery (*The Italian,* 1: 165). Though the objects of the hero's exalted emotions may be misplaced, surely he is in better state than the man who feels no such impulse whatever.

Since the spectral nature of the monk's elusiveness rests mainly in Vivaldi's subjective impressions, not in the objective phenomena, little implausible explaining away is needed. The ghostly visitations he experiences in prison require an elaborate system of secret doors and passages to explain them, but these trappings are rendered credible by the machinery of the Inquisition (or, more accurately, if we can believe in Gothic fiction's melodramatic picture of that institution—another attack on superstition, as embodied in the reputed fanatical excesses of Roman Catholicism—we can accept any number of secret passages and cryptic messengers).

Unlike the other romances mentioned in this chapter, the setting of *The Italian* (1797) is almost contemporaneous with its writing. Vivaldi's first meeting with Ellena is precisely dated in 1758, only six years before the English tourist of the frame narrative learns their story. In this case the frame is cast in the third person, focused on the consciousness of one of several "English travellers in Italy" (*The Italian*, 1: 1). This character's astonishment at the custom of sanctuary, by which even a murderer may be sheltered safely in a church, prompts a friar to offer him the manuscript of the main narrative. The Englishman's reaction to the sight of an assassin at large in a church, moreover, emphasizes the otherness of the Italian setting. Some such device is needed to foreground the remoteness of the novel's world, since here temporal distance is minimal, a matter of a generation or two (to be exact, thirty-nine years) rather than centuries. In the polarized scheme of English versus foreign, we, as implied readers, find ourselves at the "English" end of the scale. The frame itself, as always, contributes to the distance, especially since the narrative is supposed to be written not by one of the principals in the action, but by a Paduan student who "was so much struck with the facts" of Schedoni's case that he recorded the story "partly as an exercise, and partly in return for some trifling services" rendered by the friar (*The Italian*, 1: 8–9). The narrator of the main action, the supposed student of Padua, remains undramatized, so that we quickly forget his existence. He assumes, indeed, all the privileges of omniscience, shifting viewpoints freely and providing background information (e.g., Schedoni's personality traits) known to no single character within the story. On occasions of highly wrought emotion and suspense, however, the narrative remains within the consciousness of the protagonist, such as Ellena or Vivaldi, compelling the reader to share the moment-to-moment unfolding of mystery and terror. Thus we enjoy no superiority over the characters in respect to knowing the true nature of the phenomena they confront.

In contrast to the novels discussed so far, which resolve the intimations of the fantastic into the uncanny, Radcliffe's posthumous *Gaston de Blondeville* (1826) moves from the fantastic into the marvelous. Its similarity to *The Castle of Otranto* is easily recognized, for the specters in both romances appear for good purposes—to avenge old crimes. *Gaston de Blondeville*, however, contains intimations of the fantastic entirely absent from *Otranto*. The visit of a genuine ghost is prepared for by a lengthier frame than in any of Radcliffe's other novels. Two young Englishmen, who might be the author's contemporaries, are touring Kenilworth Castle. The length of the frame narrative allows scope for the pair to be somewhat individualized—Simpson, the prosaic, flippant one, and Willoughton, the romantic one (a common contrast in fiction of the period, epitomized in *Sense and Sensibility*). In Willoughton the aesthetic contemplation of the supernatural at a distance comes into play. Such sportiveness, however, has no part in the main narrative. We are less sure than in *The Italian* which side we ought to take with regard to the pair of opposite polarities represented by the two Englishmen. However, Willoughton, as transmitter of the narrative, gets the last word, though his own response, as we shall see, is not unambiguous. The castle ruins stimulate a lively debate between them on history, legend, and ghosts. During their visit to the castle's environs, they come upon an old villager who has found a buried chest full of books and manuscripts. The romantic Willoughton buys the chest and finds therein the manuscript from which he adapts the novel's main narrative. His version of the tale is not a transcription, but a "modernized copy" (*Gaston*, 1: 75).* Our only clue to the changes made by Willoughton is his own statement that he "endeavoured to preserve somewhat of the air of the old style, without its dryness" and "often retained the old words, where they did not seem to form too glaring a contrast with the modern style" (*Gaston*, 1: 75). The temporal distance produced by setting the tale in the time of Henry III is enhanced by the adaptor's implication that the medieval milieu is too alien to be appreciated without judicious modernization.

The document itself assumes greater importance in this romance than in Radcliffe's others, taking on a concrete existence as an artifact. Willoughton's narrative is divided into a series of "Days," following the plan of the original, and each is prefaced by a description of the picture that, according to the adaptor, appears at that point in the manuscript. Despite the care Willoughton takes with the use of the original document in preparing his account, he does not necessarily endorse the story. The testimony of the medieval writer lacks corroboration sufficient to convince Willoughton's eighteenth-century mind. Unlike the characters within the tale, he is in no danger of being frightened by the specter; he is free to contemplate and manipulate the discredited beliefs of a vanished era. Like the knight of Keats' "La Belle Dame sans merci," he makes only a temporary sojourn in the faerie realm. The structure of the book closes a circle, causing the reader, with Willoughton, to leave the modern world for the Gothic world, then to withdraw from that realm and return to his own. The ghost, therefore, has

---

*This edition of *Gaston de Blondeville* contains an irregularity in pagination; page numbers in volume 2 begin over again with "one" midway in the volume. The second set of page numbers will be cited as "volume 2a."

authenticated existence only within the medieval tale. The frame narrative, dissociating itself from the main story, partakes of the fantastic. The omniscient narrator of the frame suggests that "one better versed in antiquities" than Willoughton would have noticed inconsistencies that cast doubt on the manuscript's provenance. Though aware of some of these difficulties, Willoughton remains "willing to suppose" the document authentic. When the narrator attributes Willoughton's supposition (or suspension of disbelief) to "the enthusiasm of an antiquary," the eighteenth-century rationalist's suspicion of "enthusiasm" comes to mind. The young enthusiast engages in deliberate, though harmless, self-deception: "Willoughton was so willing to think he had met with a specimen of elder times, that he refused to dwell on the evidence, which went against its stated origin" (*Gaston,* 2a: 51, 53). Taking a romance-writer's position, he values the emotions evoked by the narrative regardless of the story's correspondence to fact. When he tells his skeptical friend, stirred against his will by the castle's atmosphere, "Your feelings are true to my arguments, in spite of your own" (*Gaston,* 1: 67), he clearly reveals where his allegiance lies.

What position is held by the narrator of the medieval tale, presumed to be a monk? Though the frame narrator comments on this monastic chronicler's anachronistic open-mindedness about witchcraft, the monk never *denies* the possibility of supernatural intervention in everyday life. Clauses like "whatever might pass that night in this hall, raised up by beings of another region" (*Gaston,* 2: 94) illustrate his acceptance of this possibility. As for the specter itself, he presents it as probably genuine. He writes for a reader prepared to accept the specter as genuine, just as the reader seems willing to accept and concur with the chronicler's moralizing on the transience of human life and the value of a tranquil spirit. This story has, in fact, two implied readers—the monk's contemporary, to whom the active intrusion of supernatural forces into ordinary life is a real possibility, and Willoughton's reader. The eighteenth-century transcriber, we are told, makes his modernized copy "for the amusement of a friend" (*Gaston,* 1: 75). The friend, like Willoughton himself, will be neither edified nor seriously frightened by the ghost, but only entertained by it. From the original chronicler's point of view, Willoughton, who seeks, beyond aesthetic titillation, only to learn "some new traits of an age so distant from his own" (*Gaston,* 1: 74), is not at all the proper audience for the tale. He values the quality of distance, where the original author intends the immediacy of a moral lesson. Standing on the far side of the line dividing a believing from a skeptical world view, Willoughton is free to treat the ghost aesthetically.

The monastic chronicler himself, though, makes no positive assertions about the apparition's genuineness. Even within Gaston's story, the ghost's status during its public visitations is uncertain. Seen by a number of people, it looks like an ordinary man. Its only spectral trait is a habit of frequenting presumably inaccessible places, like the gallery of a locked room, and appearing and vanishing abruptly when not under direct observation. The reader, distanced from the characters by a presumably greater sophistication, may well expect these phenomena to dissolve in a mundane explanation. The characters themselves are doubtful of the apparition's nature. Gaston first thinks it resembles his dead father, but then claims "he now knew it to have been only an apparition, suggested in his own mind" (*Gaston*, 2: 19). Note that this is the opinion Gaston *claims* to hold; the omniscient narrator does not offer us entry to Gaston's mind. Later, when the characters are convinced the mysterious figure cannot be natural, some suspect it of being not a ghost but an illusion produced by a sorcerer to discredit Gaston. "Many and divers were the opinions and sayings upon this affair," and most of a page is taken up by the buzzings of rumor on this subject (*Gaston*, 2: 258–59). Suggestiveness remains central to Radcliffe's technique; uncertainty surrounds her ghost for most of the book. When it finally visits King Henry to make its purpose plain, the conversation occurs in the King's bedchamber at night in a dreamlike atmosphere. Here the narrator distances himself furthest from his subject, repeatedly using language like "as was said," "it is said," and "that, which followed, was said to be no deceit of his fancy" (*Gaston*, 2a: 20–22). The authenticity of this ghost, after all, rests on hearsay.

As in most of these romances, of course, uncertainty is augmented by temporal displacement. Most obvious is the lapse of centuries, with an accompanying change in world view, between the medieval chronicle and Willoughton's adaptation. Within the Gaston tale, plot is displaced from story by the device of Todorov's two stories: first, the ghost's haunting of Kenilworth and the complications arising therefrom; second, revealed late in the narrative, the history of past wrongs that the specter has come to disclose. The monastic chronicler, however, manipulates time in other ways. The division of the action into eight days emphasizes the drama's encapsulation in time as well as in the confined space of the castle. In the concluding paragraphs of the eighth day, though, the narrator moves out from this temporal encapsulation to suggest vast expanses of time, a vastness that he contrasts with the brevity of individual life. Change in time scale is suggested by contemplation of the nearly deserted castle after the departure of the court. As the "vision of the living world" withdraws from Kenilworth, the narrative withdraws from the hectic eight days of the action to the "years of ordinary life" (*Gaston*, 2a: 48, 50). The narrator lengthens the time scale still further by contrasting the length of "ordinary life" with "the seeming ages of a cloistered one." He then evokes an image of a scale so large that it dwarfs any human span: "Yet even here life is still a FLEETING VISION! As such it fades . . . nor leaves a gleam behind—save of the light of good works" (*Gaston*, 2a: 50). The light metaphor forms a counterpart to the final paragraph of the frame (and of the book as a whole), when sunrise awakens Willoughton from his antiquarian reverie and causes him, "deeply affected by the almost holy serenity," to look heavenward in "blissful gratitude and adoration" (*Gaston*, 2a: 55). This correspondence between the two conclusions forms a link between the medieval and eighteenth-century world views, since, despite their differences on the subject of spectral activity, they have in common a reverence for the higher supernatural and response to its claims.

The delicate handling of the supernatural in *Gaston* is apt to impress the twentieth-century reader as far more satisfying than the rather blatant manifestations in *Otranto*. Yet *Gaston de Blondeville* contains little genuine terror, compared to *Udolpho* and *The Italian*. In the final analysis, the mundane explanations of the strange, terrific events in most of Radcliffe's romances spoil the effect less than we might suppose. As C. M. Manlove says in *Modern Fantasy*, "Those Gothic novels in which the supernatural is revealed to be some merely natural phenomenon . . . are really no different in kind from those which offer no such explanation, for in both the purpose is simply to stimulate the reader's unconscious terrors" (Manlove, 6). While I cannot agree with the simplistic generalization that the two kinds of novels are literally "no different," I do agree with Manlove that supernatural incidents in fiction elicit certain emotions independent of their rationalized or unrationalized status. By the time natural causes are uncovered, the supernatural suggestions have already done their work. These suggestions induce both protagonists and readers to consider the possible existence of the unseen world; a precise decision about the status of that world need not be reached. We have found three uses for the supposed supernatural in Radcliffe's novels: (1) to elevate the mind to the spiritual realm; (2) to caution against the dangers of superstitious fear; and (3) to produce aesthetic pleasure through contemplation of the other-worldly. (This contemplation, like the visit of Keats' knight to the realm of La Belle Dame, is of course temporary, always followed by a return to ordinary reality. Emily's fancies about fireflies have no effect on her everyday behavior, and after a night of poring over his medieval manuscript, Willoughton wakes to the light of common day.) The author controls and limits the effects of these processes upon reader and characters by eventually revealing the "supernatural" as illusory or, in the case of *Gaston*, by mediating the real ghost story through a lengthy frame in which the supernatural episodes are considered skeptically. The spirits are invoked and dismissed without being allowed to wander outside the confines of their enchanted circle.

3

Occult Conspiracies

Radcliffe, we have seen, often uses suggestions of supernatural terror to "expand the soul religiously" or, according to Peavoy, to show that innocence lies under the constant protection of the Divine. Her use of the fantastic-uncanny serves to evoke the possibility of another world without demanding belief in it, thus avoiding the hazards of superstition. Another type of Gothic fiction, however, employs the fantastic almost entirely for the latter purpose. The two novels to be discussed in this chapter raise supernatural fears in the reader (and the characters) expressly so that these fears may be dispelled. The supernatural serves the primary function of being disproved. While in Radcliffe hints of possible contact with a supernatural realm are sometimes consoling, in these two novels presumed encounters with the unseen world are almost always dreadful. Superstitious terrors are the target of the Germanic romances *Horrid Mysteries* and *The Necromancer*. Novels like these offer promise of revealing the mysteries of life and death but end by revealing the absence of mystery.*

These novels' ruthless stripping of the veil differs fundamentally from Radcliffe's gentler method because of the different responses expected from the respective readers. Playful invocation of already subdued spirits almost never occurs in *The Necromancer* and *Horrid Mysteries,* for to their authors, the threat posed by superstition is immediate and practical rather than remote and philosophical. The preface to the latter book, in particular, explicitly warns the reader against treading the hero's fatal path and takes pains to present evidence that the Illuminati are an urgent contemporary danger. A related difference between the Radcliffean Gothic and the Germanic Gothic lies in the kind of isolation suffered by the protagonists. Radcliffe's heroines are imprisoned and sometimes (e.g., Ellena in *The Italian*) falsely accused, but they experience no fundamental self-doubt. Their temporary exclusion is

---

*Such, at least, is their stated aim. *Horrid Mysteries* may be charged with some degree of failure at this goal. In this story many of the supposed supernatural events are not, in the end, explained.

externally imposed. The isolation of Carlos in *Horrid Mysteries,* on the other hand, arises from an internal source, his own confusion and paranoia. In this book as in *The Necromancer,* the complications of the multivocal narrative provide an objective correlative to the characters' bewilderment. The reader, temporarily sharing this confusion, experiences the fraudulent supernatural as a present threat. His only advantage over the hero of each story is the monitory preface that alerts him to the likelihood of fraud.

The German original of *The Necromancer,* entitled *Der Geisterbanner, eine Wundergeschichte aus mundlichen und schriftlichen Traditionem gesumnelt* [*sic*], was published in 1792. The author, Karl Friedrich Kahlert, used the pseudonym Lawrence Flammenberg. The English translation by Peter Teuthold, a German refugee in England, appeared from the Minerva Press in 1794. *Horrid Mysteries* is also a translation from a German romance, first published as *Memoirs of the Marquis de Grosse.** The Minerva Press published Peter Will's translation in 1796. Summers identifies this novel with *Der Genius,* translated in the same year by Joseph Trapp as *The Genius; or, The Mysterious Adventures of Don Carlos de Grandez.* We notice that the *Memoirs* title constitutes an explicit claim by the original author, Karl Grosse, of the story's autobiographical basis.† That *Horrid Mysteries* and *The Necromancer,* in translation, become a part of the English Gothic tradition is indicated by Jane Austen's inclusion of both in her *Northanger Abbey* list of seven "horrid" novels. As late as 1817 Thomas Love Peacock makes Scythrop, in *Nightmare Abbey,* sleep with *Horrid Mysteries* under his pillow. These two romances are of interest to us, moreover, because they form conspicuous exceptions to Peavoy's schematization of three modes of the supernatural in Gothic novels. As we shall see, the "explaining away" of the supernatural in these German tales does not demonstrate, as in Radcliffe's works, that "a world of artificial terrors is finally a secure world" (Peavoy, 110). In *Horrid Mysteries* particularly, the problematic nature of the supernatural phenomena instead reinforces an image of the universe as a bewildering, even hostile, place.

D. P. Varma maintains that the German *Schauerroman* "awakened to consciousness in an atmosphere of mental confusion and uncertainty following the collapse of an established social order" (*Horrid Mysteries,* xiv). The structure of these two examples of the subgenre mirrors the characters' confusion about metaphysical truths as well as the factual status of events impinging on their lives. In *Horrid Mysteries* the reader is apt to be at least as

---

*D.P. Varma's introduction does not give a date for the German edition, nor does Montague Summers' *Gothic Bibliography.*

†It is convenient to go on referring to Grosse as the author, as claimed on the title page, despite the problematic status of this identification of author with fictional narrator.

confused as the characters, sometimes more so. Both tales take the form of what we may call documentary novels, a more inclusive term than epistolary, since the stories are told in memoirs as well as letters. *The Necromancer* has the reassuring symmetry of a detective story (except that the explication of "what really happened" takes up much more space than in the conventional mystery of that type). The first half presents inexplicable, seemingly preternatural events through the eyes and minds of the bewildered characters enmeshed therein. Though the narrators may be unreliable in the sense that their perceptions are flawed, they are assumed to be honest reporters of their own experiences. In the second half of the book, the facts behind these experiences are systematically unveiled, with no significant detail left unaccounted for. (The veil metaphor is as relevant to these two novels as to *The Mysteries of Udolpho;* the preface of *The Necromancer* alludes to "the mysterious Veil of pretended supernatural Aid" [*The Necromancer*, xviii] and the preface of *Horrid Mysteries* to "the imposing veil of mysteriousness" [*Horrid Mysteries,* xv]. Both novels present a world in which reality is shrouded by illusion.) In this process the hero, who has gathered the documents exposing the "Necromancer," serves as the reader's surrogate within the novel. *Horrid Mysteries,* on the other hand, presents us with no such clear-cut structure. As Varma puts it, "the incidents follow in a series of apocalyptic visions" (*Horrid Mysteries,* xiii). We must follow the plot's thread through a veritable labyrinth. Nor do we have the benefit of a reliable guide. The principal narrator appears reticent, possibly disingenuous, and perhaps even morally unreliable as well. Both of these novels illustrate the "two stories" Todorov postulates for the mystery genre.

As Todorov points out, the double story, according to the Russian Formalists, characterizes every work of fiction. The story is always distinct from the plot of a narrative; "the story is what has happened in life, the plot is the way the author presents it to us" (Todorov, *The Poetics of Prose,* 45). The plot may involve temporal inversion, condensation of long stretches of time into brief summary, reversal of the order of cause and effect, and many other dislocations of the "natural" process of events. Along the lines of Shklovsky's notorious claim that *Tristram Shandy* is the most typical of English novels, we might make a case for *Horrid Mysteries* as the most typical of Gothic novels. Whether by design or carelessness, it carries the dislocation of narrative to almost Shandean lengths. I shall first discuss the less radical dislocations of the earlier *Necromancer* (English version, 1794).

This novel shares with *Horrid Mysteries* the motif of fradulent supernatural phenomena deliberately manufactured by a band of conspirators. In *The Necromancer* the "ghosts" are a gang of robbers protecting their hideout with the help of what would be called, in later periods, a spurious medium. Both novels differ from the typical English Gothic of the Radcliffe school by focusing on the consciousness of a male rather than a female protagonist. *The Necromancer* begins with an undramatized, omniscient narrator's account of the meeting of two friends, Herrman and Hellfried, after many years' separation. Though the date of the original adventure of the haunted castle is 1750, the story is not told until the 1770s, so that the characteristic Gothic distance is achieved by the placing of Herrman and Hellfried's adventures in their own past, recalled in nostalgic tranquility around a fireside. With the question "Dost thou believe in spirits?" Hellfried introduces his tale of a strange experience, connected with the theft and recovery of his watch, that befell him during his wanderings (*The Necromancer*, 6). By the sort of coincidence typical of Gothic novels, one that imitates fate, Herrman also has a weird experience to relate, apparently connected with Hellfried's. Herrman tells his tale in part orally and in part through a collection of documents he gives to his friend for later perusal. The rest of the book, after part 1 (the conversations between Herrman and Hellfried, comprising only thirty-seven pages), consists entirely of mediated narrative.

Herrman appears anxious to authenticate his tale of the apparitions he witnessed in a ruined, reputedly haunted castle. He makes a point of stating that his oral reminiscence covers "only that part of those adventures in which he had been personally concerned" (*The Necromancer*, 17). For the rest of the story he has assembled letters and memoirs containing first-person testimony from people who participated in the events. The author scrupulously accounts for the way each of these affidavits was acquired. Baron R—, who shared the adventure with Herrman, writes a letter to Herrman, describing an unexpected meeting with the former Lieutenant (now Major) B—, another participant in the ghostly encounter. Enclosed in the Baron's letter is a manuscript of Lieutenant B—'s first-person narrative of his role in the further investigations of the truth behind the "necromancer" Volkert. Within this written narrative are transcribed several incidents orally narrated by acquaintances of the writer. One such anecdote of Volkert's spiritualist activities, told by an Austrian veteran, contains the interpolated story of an old woman victimized by Volkert. In part 3 (a continuation of the Lieutenant's manuscript), after the capture of Volkert and the rescue of the Lieutenant's missing servant, John, the writer transcribes the interpolated oral narratives of John, Volkert, and Wolf (one of the necromancer's accomplices). Wolf's confession, however, breaks off before Lieutenant B— can hear all of it. He gets a copy of its conclusion, therefore, in a letter from a friend who happens to be present. Aside from the convention of incredibly long and detailed oral narratives reported verbatim (which this author does not unduly abuse), the nested stories and shifts from narrator to narrator are not hard to follow and carry the tale forward efficiently. The familiar device of designating persons and places only by initials supports the illusion of a true story whose exact source must be concealed "to protect the innocent." Like many another eighteenth-century author of epistolary fiction masquerading as an editor, the translator, Teuthold, maintains, "The strange mysterious Events which occur in this little Performance are founded on Facts, the authenticity of which can be warranted by the Translator" (*The Necromancer,* xviii).

Though exhibiting diffidence about the literary quality of his translation, the writer of the preface prescribes definitively how the reported events should be interpreted. Radcliffe provides no comparable commentator purporting to stand outside the text, inhabiting the "real" universe of the reader. Hermeneutic guidance in her books comes from dramatized narrators (like the introducer of *A Sicilian Romance*), reliable characters (like the governess in the same novel), or, at the most impersonal, an undramatized omniscient narrator *within* the text. In Flammenberg's novel the strange events are explicitly classified as "Frauds, perpetrated under the mysterious Veil of pretended supernatural Aid" (*The Necromancer,* xviii). If the translator's preface be considered an integral part of the novel, then we as readers are privy to the truth from the outset, and for us the tale is not fantastic, but uncanny. In what mode, though, are events presented within the story? What is their status in the thoughts and discourse of the characters? We recall that Hellfried introduces the story with a question about belief in apparitions. His own experience has left him in doubt on this point, and Herrman's tale, with all its supporting documents, is meant to answer the question. The reader identifies with Hellfried, whose doubts we share until the facts are uncovered. Within the tale Herrman offers no clear hints of the forthcoming naturalistic denouement. Lieutenant B—, however, is convinced that the ghosts are imposters, and in his first-person narrative the possibility of genuine haunting is purely formal. The local people dwelling near the haunted castle accept the ghosts without question; typical is the landlord of the inn, who tells his guests the legend of the castle's spectral lord and implores them not to trespass in the ruins. The more sophisticated travelers react with varying degrees of skepticism. The Lieutenant responds in a humorous tone that "all ghosts and hobgoblins have ever been kept at a respectful distance by a martial dress." Herrman, less certain of the unreality of ghosts, objects to the expedition, "not knowing who those spirits might be" (*The Necromancer,* 21). The Baron, too, is not prepared to agree with the Lieutenant that "all was either deceit or the effects of a deluded fancy," but insists that "one ought not to speak lightly of these matters." The latter caution suggests that, even if these particular spirits turn out to be fraudulent, in other circumstances real ghosts may exist. The heroes continue for some time to refer to the castle's inhabitants as spirits, though sometimes in a satirical rather than credulous tone. The boldness of the heroes' repeated visits to the ruin leads the simple villagers to regard them as "strange conjurors" and "supernatural beings" (*The Necromancer*, 29). Since we know the travelers are none of these things, calling them by such titles ironically undercuts the reliability of the local people who believe so firmly in the ghosts. The notion of ghosts becomes more respectable when the venerable Austrian veteran tells Lieutenant B— that "apparitions of supernatural beings ought not wholly to be rejected" (*The Necromancer*, 46), but this character's credibility is undermined by the fact that he bases his belief on an episode in which he was deceived by Volkert. Even after hearing the Austrian's story, Lieutenant B— is certain that Volkert and his "ghosts" are imposters. B— lets this opinion slip out on page 63, after which he consistently operates on the assumption of fraud. There is little room for doubt, moreover, that the fraud is a self-serving, criminal plot. Sympathies of the authoritative characters, and thus the reader, remain with the socially sanctioned forces of law (for instance, the military); the righteousness of these powers and the wickedness of the Necromancer remain unchallenged. (We shall see that the situation in *Horrid Mysteries* is a good deal more ambiguous.)

The book's avowed purpose of exposing malicious imposture leaves little or no room for the positive values of the imagined supernatural. The only link between ghosts and the spiritual world in the higher sense is made, perhaps, by the credulous landlord. He tries to dissuade the travelers from entering the ruined castle on the ground that "the devil would make us smart for our foolhardiness and unbelief" (*The Necromancer*, 21). It is unclear whether the "unbelief" is disbelief in the particular haunting or an atheistic disregard of the whole spiritual realm. The protagonists are more apt to invoke higher powers in contexts that discredit the supposed ghosts. (We recall that Radcliffe, also, often has her more reliable characters assert that the virtuous have nothing to fear from the ghostly realm.) For instance, the imposter Wolf must "prepare to meet that eternal Judge who sooner or later overtakes the wicked in his vile pursuits" (*The Necromancer*, 158). Reason and faith alike take their stand on the side of rational disbelief in apparitions.

Horrid Mysteries ostensibly attempts to convey a similar message. In practice its ambiguities—or confusions—interfere with its stated aim. The translator's preface consists of a capsule history of the Illuminati and a warning against the dangers of all secret societies "that pretend to reform the defects of government, while selfish views are concealed under the imposing outside of philanthropy and patriotism" (*Horrid Mysteries*, xviii). Like Teuthold, the translator of *Horrid Mysteries* claims that his romance is true, the factual confession of Marquis Carlos de G—, a former member of the Illuminati who has discerned their deceit and corruption and repents having "sacrificed the best time of his life in hunting after a deluding phantom" (*Horrid Mysteries*, xviii). The preface prepares us to read the novel as a cautionary tale and to expect a detailed revelation of the society's impostures. The final sentence of the preface, however, gives warning that the second expectation may be disappointed:

> Finally, the Translator thinks it needful to observe, that if the mysterious events occurring in the subsequent volumes, are not elucidated with that tiresome minuteness which renders many of our modern novels rather tedious than interesting, he flatters himself that the judicious readers will not be displeased at his confidence in their own ingenuity, which sufficiently will be enabled, by the hints the author has dropt to that purpose, to dispel the mystic gloom which he has been prevented to remove by the truth of Voltaire's words: Le Secret d'en nuyer [*sic*] est le secret de tout dire. (*Horrid Mysteries,* xviii)

As we shall see, Carlos, the protagonist of this novel, can hardly be accused of telling all. Somewhat like Tristram Shandy, he invites the reader to become his co-worker in constructing the story. The translator's remark on the "tiresome minuteness" of Gothic fiction exhaustively rationalized, hints at an enjoyment of "mystic gloom" for its own sake, absent from *The Necromancer.* Though inveighing against the poisonous effects of secrecy, the translator approves of Carlos' keeping certain secrets of his own. And although the secret society in *Horrid Mysteries* wields its corrupt power chiefly by playing on the fear of the supernatural, one of its original purposes, ironically, was to "dispel the dark clouds of superstition" (*Horrid Mysteries,* xv).

The Necromancer centers upon a conspiracy of sorts, a deception perpetrated on the public by a band of outlaws. This conspiracy is geographically limited and, once unearthed, easily uprooted and destroyed. It is antisocial, and the representatives of established authority stand solidly against it. In the world of *Horrid Mysteries,* on the other hand, conspiracy pervades all of society and encompasses men from all ranks, even, "several Princes" and "first geniuses of our age, philosophers and statesmen" (*Horrid Mysteries,* xvi). In this view the Secret Tribunal is not a mere aberrant offshoot of society as a whole, but the force that covertly dominates the whole. This attitude characterizes what Richard Hofstadter calls the "paranoid style," which centers on the belief in "a vast, insidious, preternaturally effective international conspiratorial network designed to perpetrate acts of the most fiendish character" (*Horrid Mysteries,* 14).* Those who write in this idiom often feel dispossessed, as if their country "has largely been taken away from them and their kind, though they are determined to try to repossess it" (Hofstadter, 23). Just such desperate defensiveness characterizes the preface to *Horrid Mysteries;* the translator strives to convey an urgent warning

---

*This essay is a revised version of the Herbert Spencer Lecture delivered at Oxford in November 1963.

against a monster threatening to devour what remains of his world. In this process, as in Hofstadter's cases from American history, the defector from the conspiracy assumes special importance. Almost a third of the preface consists of a statement quoted from a former member of the Illuminati, and Carlos' entire narrative is presented as the revelation of a defector (in the beginning, at least; later the book contradicts itself on this point).

Carlos, therefore, is initially presented as doubly a defector, first from the world's established order to the secret society, then from the secret society itself. As we have already noted, the fiction we are discussing arises in a period when universally accepted beliefs about physical and human nature no longer prevail. It has been said that by the late eighteenth century, "the disintegration of cosmic orders widely felt as true was finally completed" (Wasserman, *The Subtler Language*, 170). In the Romantic movement this dearth of fixed standards is expressed in the emergence of an alienated hero, at odds with his culture rather than expressing its highest values, like the heroes of earlier literature. Northrop Frye refers to this phenomenon as "the Romantic rejection of the social process as the center of human reality" (Frye, *A Study of English Romanticism*, 65). Carlos fits the pattern of the alienated character, as he seems unable to find contentment either in the larger society or in the Illuminati. In the beginning society as it is seems to represent "the false identity of the conforming group" (Frye, 47), which the Illuminati promise to replace or transform. Later, however, when Carlos turns against the conspiracy, it assumes the role of monstrous oppressor and we recall the translator's claim that several Princes belong to it. For some time Carlos isolates himself, rejecting social structure altogether in the company of a saintly hermit, seeking what Frye calls the "creative and healing alienation to be gained from a solitary contact with the order of nature outside society" (Frye, 47). When he does return to the world, Carlos, instead of appealing to the established authorities for a political solution to the problem of the Illuminati, forms a private counterconspiracy.

After summarizing the main incidents of Carlos' history and commenting on some of the novel's strengths and deficiencies, I shall outline the narrative structure—plot as opposed to story—that serves as a vehicle for these adventures. The rest of the chapter will explore the attitude (or rather, various conflicting attitudes) toward the supernatural implicit in Carlos' memoir and the interpolated tales. Carlos' story is violently dislocated from its plot; he begins in the middle, returns to the beginning, and moves on to an inconclusive end. In the first chapter he warns us of this peculiarity and justifies it: "I must, however, observe, that the course of my history is too rapid, and too complicated, to be plain in the beginning. I shall, therefore, commence with that period which begins to throw some light upon it. All the antecedent occurrences of my life do not only concentre, but are also repeated therein" (*Horrid Mysteries,* 3). The suggestion of a cyclical process puts us on guard not to count on a tidy resolution to the mysteries. Stripped of subplots, the major events of Carlos' history—as he perceives them at least—are as follows: As a young man he falls in love with Elmira. Though warned against Carlos by an anonymous letter, she agrees to elope with him. Shortly after their marriage, she mysteriously dies. Carlos suspects a secret confederacy of being involved in her death. A friend, Don Pedro, introduces him to the secret society, and Carlos is persuaded to become a member. While under the control of the society, he is seduced, with little reluctance, by a female member (or victim?), Rosalia. Separated from her, he falls out with Pedro over the affection of Pedro's wife, Francisca. Back at his own home, Carlos receives a visit from Elmira, who is, unaccountably, not dead after all. At this point he is first visited by Amanuel, the guardian spirit assigned to him by the society. Supernatural persecution causes Carlos and Elmira to flee, and she is shot to death by an unknown attacker. Attempting to escape the society's vigilance, Carlos leaves home in disguise and becomes a wanderer. During his travels he stays for awhile at a haunted castle and later lives with a venerable hermit until the old man's death. Carlos finally returns home and enters politics, but the return of Amanuel drives him to set out again. On this journey he coincidentally finds Elmira, once again restored to life, with a child! Both wife and child eventually die, not before Elmira has told Carlos some of her history, including the treachery of Pedro. (We wait expectantly for Elmira to reappear again, but this time she remains dead.) Carlos reenters society and joins with some noble friends in an attempt to oppose the secret confederacy with an organization of their own. Carlos, though, eventually marries Adelheid, who has some connection with the confederacy, and begins to consider it less evil than he had supposed. After an episode of conflict with Adelheid, they are reconciled and settle down to what may be assumed to be a life of tranquil wedded love.

That the plot wrenches this story out of temporal sequence and makes it hard to follow does not necessarily make the book bad; the same difficulties attend *Tristram Shandy.* The flaws of *Horrid Mysteries* lie in other directions. The text is apparently intended to arouse the reader to emotional sympathy with the horror and mystery of Carlos' ordeals. As indicated by the translator's preface, the conspiracy is presented as a living threat to the reader (unlike Radcliffe's ghosts). But in many instances neither character nor scene are realized fully enough to engage our emotions. Of Carlos' three wives, Elmira and Rosalia are hardly distinguishable, and Adelheid is differentiated only by constant references to her innocence and sisterly sweetness. All the characters speak in melodramatic rhetoric at moments of stress and in lengthy, didactic sentences in expository passages. The speech of peasants and servants does not differ from that of the nobly-born; a "shabby beggar" can speak to the disguised Carlos of a man who "lives in a constant round of pleasures" and a lady who "leads a very retired life" (*Horrid Mysteries,* 156). The difficulties of the narrative structure are compounded by occasional carelessness in presentation; for example, near the beginning of chapter 2 in volume 3 (*Horrid Mysteries,* 199), the author gives no typographical indication when he ends a manuscript and returns to autobiographical commentary. Though many scenes are indeed embellished with strikingly sensuous detail, and the horrific incidents feature an ample allowance of blood, groans, fire, lightning, and thunder, stylistic defects frequently obtrude themselves upon the reader's awareness. Characters are often described in terms of clichés such as "dimpled cheeks," "angelic looks," and "languishing, breathless lips" (*Horrid Mysteries,* 17, 23, 49). Most damaging are lapses, amid the height of supernatural awe, into a flatness that verges on the ludicrous. For example, at the first appearance of the supposed spirit Amanuel, after a build-up that includes an "ice cold hand," "secret horror," and "radiant splendor," Carlos concludes, "A low rustling announced to me the approach of a superior being" (*Horrid Mysteries,* 13). An egregious instance of such a lapse is the use of the incongruous verb "ambled" in the following remark: "An invisible being ambled through the apartment" (*Horrid Mysteries,* 89). (This unrationalized "invisible being," by the way, is one of the most damaging contradictions to the original thesis that all supernatural events are mere deception.) This novel presents us with narrative dislocation in a sort of chemical purity, unmixed with the distractions of literary genius.

A brief outline of the narrative pattern is in order: Setting aside the translator's preface, we find that the overall frame of the story consists of Carlos' memoirs, looking back over the "mazy labyrinths" of "the path I went, or, rather, was led" (*Horrid Mysteries,* 3). The memoir begins with a meeting between Carlos and his friend Count S—, the counterpart of the situation at the opening of *The Necromancer.* The Count tells a tale of a mysterious experience in which he encountered a lady named Francisca. Recognizing the name, Carlos realizes that the Count's history is entangled with his own. The Count's tale stimulates Carlos to narrate his own story. He begins with an oral recitation, which is broken off to return to the main narrative of the interaction between Carlos and the Count. Carlos continues the tale of his earlier life in a written account directed to Count S—. This manuscript-within-a-memoir contains an interpolated story by a cottager named James, whose past is entwined with the secret society. After James' story, a brief intermission precedes the return to Carlos' manuscript written for the Count. Thus the action of the present (Carlos' relationship with S—) develops concurrently with the unfolding of the past. The very act of retracing his past seems to bring Carlos' paranoia to the surface, for he comes to distrust Count

S— and eventually to regard him as an enemy. Within the remainder of Carlos' manuscript are several interpolated narratives. A beggar tells the disguised Carlos what popular rumor knows of his (Carlos') history, a recital that helps to shape the protagonist's decision about whether to return home and make himself known. Carlos tells his own experiences to one Mr. de B—, who receives the tale with amused disbelief. Elmira tells the sad history of her brother, thereby confirming Carlos' suspicions of Don Pedro's treachery. She then writes down her experiences while supposed dead, but the paper is destroyed when she dies again. Carlos must reconstruct the facts from what he remembers of her written testimony. His consequent uncertainty about Elmira's fate contributes to his continuing hostility toward the secret society. His manuscript, comprising about half the book, concludes with Elmira's final death, after which the novel keeps to Carlos' main narrative and proceeds in chronological order. A sense of fluidity and inconclusiveness is produced by the juncture in volume 4 where Carlos finishes his life story in chapter 4 but reluctantly resumes it in chapter 5. The final, one-paragraph chapter of the book implies that the story is still not ended, but only suspended: "I do, indeed, not flatter myself that fate will suffer me to proceed in sweet tranquillity on my pilgrimage to a better world; however, as the future events of my life, probably, will be similar to my past adventures, I shall not trouble the patience of my friends by a communication of them" (*Horrid Mysteries*, 358). Although the open-ended quality of this nonconclusion at first brings Sterne to mind, closer examination reveals more contrast than similarity. *Tristram Shandy*, unlike Carlos, announces his resolution to go on writing new volumes of his history as long as he lives. And whereas Carlos anticipates future experiences of a monotonous predictability, Tristram boasts (for instance, in volume 4, chapter 32) that his readers will be unable to guess the future course of his tale. Carlos' introductory chapter expresses a hope that he has attained freedom from the "invisible web" ensnaring him (*Horrid Mysteries*, 3); his concluding statement makes it clear that he has not. His uncertain tranquillity still depends on fate; his life is not in his own control. Whether by human conspirators, supernatural forces, or the "Superior Power" itself, his destiny continues to be manipulated (*Horrid Mysteries*, 3). In contrast to the impression of spontaneity produced by *Tristram Shandy*, Carlos' history appears characterized by determinism. Hence the futility of narrating any more of a sequence whose endless repetition the protagonist is powerless to prevent.

What attitude toward the supernatural does this convoluted plot convey? Several spirits appear, some explained, others accounted for partly or not at all. The least definite is an apparition of Elmira enjoyed by Carlos (at a time, by the way, when she is not really dead). In a nocturnal reverie he penetrates "to the world where Elmira resided, where she awaited me, hoarding up joys unspeakable for her Carlos" (*Horrid Mysteries,* 141). He imagines himself in her embrace, the reward for his increase in virtue. (At this period he is living with the saintly hermit.) He then seems to see "Elmira's spirit throning on a silver cloud," transfigured from woman to angel. Though he uses the words "fancy" and "imagination" to characterize his vision, he nevertheless finds religious consolation in it—"eternity represented itself before my flowery imagination, with its numerous train of never-fading blessings" (*Horrid Mysteries,* 142, 141). Here supernatural phenomena and spiritual or even mystical experience are clearly connected. The possibly imaginary nature of the vision (as in Radcliffe's novels) does not detract from the value of the feelings engendered. The validity of the quasi-epiphany, however, is retrospectively undermined not only by Elmira's reappearance in living form, but also by Carlos' subsequent behavior. After the hermit's death, Carlos similarly believes himself favored by intercourse with a higher realm: "The night was the only time when I was left to myself; and I devoted it entirely to the conversation with my sainted friend, repeating in silent ecstasy his valuable principles and rules. I believed to hear his spirit when the nocturnal breezes shook the leaves of the chestnut-tree, and was everywhere haunted by a mystic sensation of his presence" (*Horrid Mysteries,* 154). We cannot tell whether Carlos' sense of the hermit's guardian presence corresponds to anything real. The subjectivity of his mystical experience is here a virtue; we can enjoy the thrill and consolation of contact with the spiritual world without being required either to accept or to reject it. His period of retirement with the hermit seems to represent an attempt to find peace and truth in solitary communion with nature. After death the hermit becomes a sort of benevolent *genius loci.* The paternal ghost's effect on Carlos is short-lived, though: "I returned, however, to the realms of reality before a month was elapsed.... I began to be less frequently reminded of him" (*Horrid Mysteries,* 154). Once removed from the location inhabited by his good genius, Carlos soon ceases to be reminded at all. The reference to reality both implies that the ghostly comfort is an illusion and foreshadows Carlos' abandonment of the pure principles he has embraced as the hermit's disciple.

A quite different kind of ghost story appears in volume 3, chapter 3, as an anecdote narrated by Carlos' friend, the Count. Like *The Necromancer,* this tale concerns a haunting actually engineered by a band of robbers. The reader is not allowed to seriously entertain the idea of a ghost, since the Count avows from the beginning that he gives "very little credit to the apparition of ghosts" (*Horrid Mysteries,* 211). His tone throughout signals a humorous rather than horrific denouement in the offing. The ghost itself, an "enormous figure, with large, fiery eyes," is too "grotesque" and "extravagant" to be frightening, and the Count analyzes it quite coolly (*Horrid Mysteries,* 212). The Count focuses mainly on the laughable cowardice exhibited by a member of the ghost-hunting party. This anecdote is a lesson in how not to generate spectral terror and serves as a comic foil to the mysterious horrors assailing Carlos elsewhere in the book. And precipitating a quarrel that destabilizes the counter-conspiracy, this incident also functions to rescue the story from a detour into comedy of manners and restore the occult emphasis. The apparitions of Amanuel, Carlos' guardian spirit, though said to be equally spurious, are subtler; Amanuel is not described except as a "transparent airy being," and the sounds, atmospheric disturbances, and lighting effects that accompany his visits seem an attempt to surround him with some aura of the numinous. Carlos testifies that at his first meeting with Amanuel the apparition is "convincing" and "could not have been the illusion of a dream" and that "my whole belief in the non-existence of spirits was, of course, violently shaken" (*Horrid Mysteries,* 86). We are not told, unfortunately, what becomes of Carlos' belief in the supernatural when, in volume 4, chapter 1, Amanuel is revealed (at the point of death) as Carlos' long-lost uncle, disguised all these years as Carlos' faithful servant Alfonso. This double disguise does not explain how the false Amanuel managed to produce all the inexplicable phenomena that attended his apparitions. The icy chills and the like could be Carlos' subjective impression, but surely not the "transparent, airy" appearance. Alfonso claims to have left papers that reveal all, but we are not allowed to see them. Though the effect of the earlier scenes need not be obliterated by their inconsistency with the denouement, we cannot help feeling cheated by this gap. It seems that the author either has forgotten what he wrote in the first volume or hopes the reader has.

The protagonist's attitudes toward the secret society change with equally bewildering discontinuity. At Alfonso-Amanuel's death, when Carlos recognizes the creature he has formerly dreaded as his guardian angel, he still calls the society "that dreadful confederation." Though Adelheid has been trying to moderate his hatred of the society, so far she has barely succeeded in subduing his "aversion from its principles" (*Horrid Mysteries,* 276, 269). Yet as soon as Alfonso reveals himself as not only Carlos' uncle but as the actual head of the confederation, with stunning suddenness Carlos embraces membership in the society as life's greatest treasure. He speaks with warmhearted approval of a fellow novice, Don Bernhard, who "hated and scorned men, merely to be able to relieve them more effectually; and being obdurated against tears and sufferings, proceeded over ruins and bleeding corpses towards his great mark of perfection" (*Horrid Mysteries,* 281–82). Is the author perpetrating irony here? The wholehearted friendship between Bernhard and the hero makes that interpretation implausible. Nor does Bernhard seem to fit the role of the conventional eighteenth-century "benevolent misanthrope," who takes a pessimistic view of mankind's moral capacity but shows charity toward individuals.* Instead, Carlos' friend seems to profess a love for humanity in general that is belied by his behavior in particular cases. Carlos' lack of repulsion at this paradoxical fusion of hate and mercy is rendered more puzzling by the fact that his distrust of this ruthless pragmatism has been his chief objection to the confederacy all along. But as Hofstadter points out, purveyors of the paranoid style share with their imagined conspirators a readiness to embrace any means that may advance the overarching end. The initiation of Don Bernhard and Adelheid is portrayed as an ecstatic feast of harmony and even Rosalia, identified a few pages earlier as destructive and vengeful, is mysteriously present and welcome. At this point the established order is once again the oppressor, while the secret confederation offers what Frye describes (in the work of Shelley) as a "gnosis," a "secret, perilous, and forbidden knowledge, like that of Adam in Eden, snatched from under the nose of a jealous Jupiter" (Frye, 106). The initiation ceremony concludes in terms that suggest the society's supernatural aura may not, after all, be entirely a fraud: "Unspeakable, mystic rites commenced; celestial sounds struck our ears with rapture; heavenly visions astonished our gazing eyes; all presensions were accomplished, and the boldest hopes silenced by reality" (*Horrid Mysteries,* 296). Here, strangely enough, reality means not the familiar experience of mundane life (as in the aftermath of the hermit's death) but the very manifestations the novel was originally supposed to discredit. By this point we wonder what has become of the book's monitory function. Are we to join Carlos in his revised opinion of the Illuminati? Or does the editor obliquely present the hero's radical shift of attitude as a terrifying instance of the conspiracy's seductive power? If so, he furnishes no cues to that effect.

The character of Carlos makes it difficult to accept any assessment he makes as finally valid. Not only does he change his mind about the confederacy several times, he is still more fickle toward the women in his life. Besides Elmira, Rosalia, and Adelheid, before his last marriage he becomes entangled in brief intrigues with Francisca and Caroline, the wife and beloved (respectively) of two friends of his. Why should we believe in the permanence of any commitment Carlos makes? He even conceives a violent jealousy of Adelheid, though they are reconciled by the end of the novel. This episode, in which he spies on his wife like an Othello without the excuse of an Iago's prompting, is only an illustration of the paranoia he has displayed throughout the story. Justifiably or not, his connection with the society leads him to see a terrible and secret significance in everything that happens to him.

---

*See Thomas R. Preston, *Not in Timon's Manner: Feeling, Misanthropy, and Satire in Eighteenth-Century England.*

In Paris, while he and his friends are trying to maintain their own counterconspiracy, Carlos blames every reverse they suffer, even love affairs and separations that seem to bear no relation to their plots, on the machinations of the society. This counterconspiracy conforms to another pattern typical of the paranoid style—imitation of the enemy. The sinister, quasi-demonic foe becomes "a projection of the self" to which "both the ideal and the unacceptable aspects of the self are attributed" (Hofstadter, 32). Obsession with hierarchy and ceremony of the secret conspiracy leads to acting out a parody of them (for instance, the vestments and ritual of the Ku Klux Klan). On an individual level, Carlos proves himself as amoral as he accuses his persecutors of being. He even exchanges roles with them somewhat as Caleb Williams, in Godwin's study of persecution, does with Falkland. Like Carlos, the narrator of *Things as They Are, or, the Adventures of Caleb Williams* (1794) finds himself persecuted by all men. The only organized society that will accept him is a band of highwaymen (analogous to Carlos' extralegal confederation). He is forced to abandon even this refuge; by the end of his story he is utterly friendless (in this respect more extremely alienated than Carlos). The epitome of isolation and alienation, he comes to believe that appealing to the officially constituted legal system is the act of a coward. Carlos seems to hold similar beliefs since instead of turning to the law to suppress the conspiracy, he opposes the Illuminati by means of a freely chosen band of friends.

Further on he makes the revealing remark, "I was constantly surrounded by members of secret societies, and enthusiasts of all sorts, got possession of their secrets, and observed that they were far inferior to what I already knew" (*Horrid Mysteries,* 199). If not a simple statement of fact, this claim indicates an obsession verging on clinical paranoia (or, if not that, then the institutionalized paranoia described by Hofstadter). An obstacle to accepting the former alternative is the tone of the novel's first chapter, introducing Carlos' memoir with a retrospective glance over his whole life. He does not write like a man who has found peace in joyful acceptance of a previously misunderstood brotherhood, but like a man persecuted:

> The invisible web, which encompassed my fate, is now, perhaps, torn asunder; and perhaps not. While I fancy to be free, the fetters which I imagine to have shaken off, are, perhaps, forged stronger, and may soon enthral me again.... Every action of my life seems to me to have been computed and arranged in their dreadful archives before I was born; they are all directed, in a preconcerted manner, towards the most horrid crime, to the perpetration of which they wanted to seduce me. (*Horrid Mysteries,* 3)

What this unspeakable crime is, we are never told. This lacuna suits the overall tone of the passage, which embodies conjecture and supposition. The recurrence of words like "perhaps," "may" and "seems" marks the writer's mental state, explicitly described by the verbs "fancy" and "imagine." And since our only contact with the reality of the novel is mediated through Carlos' memories, the pervasive murkiness characterizes the fictional universe as well as the narrative style. One thing about this universe is clear though—it is a deterministic one, ruled by fate. The narrator has no significant freedom of action; the frequent use of passive voice reinforces the imagery of web and fetters. Most chilling is the declaration, "Every action of my life seems to me to have been computed and arranged in their dreadful archives." Whether or not the secret society really arranged Carlos' life, someone did—the author. This passage covertly presents the secret society as a surrogate for the author. Whatever horrid crime the conspiracy (or the author) has in mind for Carlos, it never transpires. And perhaps even he, in his paranoia, does not actually know this ultimate secret. But Carlos is, in fact, reticent from the beginning; he reacts strongly to the tale of Count S— in the second chapter but does not tell us the reasons for his excitement until some time later. Is Carlos honest or disingenuous, sane or mad? Is the secret society good or evil? Do their claims of occult knowledge and power have any foundation in fact? The ambiguities that make these questions unanswerable constitute either irony so subtle it defeats itself or plain ineptitude.

On a first reading of the early chapters, the suggestions of ineffable horror and the impending penetration of the veil between this world and another can produce their designed effect. But the final disappointment of the expectations thus raised washes backward, as it were, to vitiate the impact of the "horrid" scenes. Why does the attempted explaining away spoil *Horrid Mysteries* but not Radcliffe's romances? The very incompleteness of the rationalization, perhaps, is a contributing factor. In the face of continuing hints of the other-worldly (for instance, in Carlos' and Adelheid's initiation ceremony), the proferred material causes constitute an annoying distraction. Ideally the discourse of the fantastic maintains a suspension between natural and supernatural world views. *Horrid Mysteries,* on the contrary, lays the two models side by side and, instead of allowing us to entertain both simultaneously, forces us to leap abruptly from one to the other. The uncertainty generated by Carlos' disingenuousness, as well as the mélange of inconsistent testimony he incorporates into his confession, remains radically unresolved. The inconsistencies in the facts of the story may arise from a conflict between the book's stated aim to expose secret societies and the desire to horrify. The author seems to create the most blood-curdling and inexplicable events he can imagine, then finds himself embarrassed when required to justify them.

It is interesting that a romance designed to expose occult fraud, an endeavor that should bring comfort to a rational mind, ends in the bleakness of Carlos' inconclusive and perhaps temporary wedded happiness. Romances like Radcliffe's, with their contrasting attitude toward the imagined supernatural, end with a definite comic resolution. In Peavoy's terms, they resemble nightmares, whose terrors prove illusory upon waking. Radcliffe's universe is ultimately benevolent; a good will underlies it. The will behind the universe of *Horrid Mysteries* must be capricious or malign. For this world a sinister conspiracy is indeed a suitable metaphor. *Horrid Mysteries* foreshadows the pessimism of novels like *Melmoth the Wanderer,* the subject of the next chapter. Grosse's novel also looks forward to Lytton's *A Strange Story,* which, like much nineteenth-century fiction in this field, similarly attempts to rationalize the occult without stripping away its mystery.

4

Faustian Wanderers

The two previous chapters have examined two ways in which eighteenth-century Gothic fiction deals with the imagined supernatural. Radcliffe's romances entertain the allure of the unseen world without committing themselves to actual superstition, while the Germanic horror-tales chiefly exhibit the hazards of flirtation with belief in that world. In Charles Robert Maturin's *Melmoth the Wanderer* (1820) we meet the supernatural unrationalized. A comparison of this novel with its near contemporary *Frankenstein* (1818) will be instructive. Though Mary Shelley's novel is more properly defined as science fiction than supernatural fantasy, since Frankenstein supposedly instills life into the monster by means of hitherto undiscovered principles of nature, the absence of any explanation of these principles surrounds his creation with an aura of magic. And Frankenstein, significantly, receives his first inspiration from occultists (so characterized by Frankenstein's professor, M. Krempe) like Cornelius Agrippa, Albertus Magnus, and Paracelsus, rather than "legitimate" scientists. Frye points out that at this period, among other "ancient superstitions, the making of homunculi...took on a new significance as symbolizing the kind of knowledge, whether fascinating or merely sinister, that man might obtain through his renewed contact with the mysteries of nature" (Frye, 69). As we shall see, moreover, the young scientist, despite his ostensibly rationalistic world view, perceives his work not as legitimate investigation but as an unnatural invasion of a forbidden realm. The consequences of his creative act waken him to a supernatural source of value that he seems to have previously ignored. *Frankenstein* resembles modern science fiction less than it resembles Victorian attempts to reconcile occultism with science, like the works of Lytton. In the fiction so far discussed, we have noted hesitation between two alternative explanations of strange phenomena: (a) the phenomena are genuine and genuinely supernatural; or (b) the supposed supernatural events are actually natural phenomena, illusions or hoaxes. Many nineteenth-century tales, however, tacitly hold in suspension three possibilities: (a) the phenomena are in fact supernatural; (b) they are natural, and the subject is a victim of deceit or delusion; or (c) the events are outside the boundaries of nature as we know it but are not supernatural in the traditional sense—the true explanation lies in scientific laws yet unknown to the majority of men. The latter phenomena might better be called preternatural. Frankenstein's creature best fits into the third category. Both *Frankenstein* and *Melmoth* display complexity in the use of mediated narrative to support an ambiguous treatment of the supernatural or preternatural. Both novels focus on the reliability of narrative; Frankenstein's story is filtered through a biased informant, while in *Melmoth* the truth can be found only by sifting through a variety of documents and hearsay reports. In these stories, more than the facts of the case, the actuality of the reported events, hangs in doubt. Ambiguity enshrouds the value of knowledge, the moral status of characters and actions, the very existence of objective good and evil, and the possibility of the characters' comprehending the universe in which they dwell. Among the questions explicitly or implicitly raised are: Is knowledge as such necessarily a good? Is there such a thing as forbidden knowledge (forbidden by some superhuman agency)? In a world infected by Original Sin, can any deed remain untainted by evil? Must good intentions inexorably go wrong? Or, in Melmoth's case, can evil intent involuntarily be shaped toward good ends? Is human society as a whole implicated in the "villainy" of Melmoth and the monster? Both authors reinforce this theme of interdependence by setting up a series of characters whose roles echo each other, i.e., Walton–Frankenstein–the monster–Justine, and John–Melmoth–Stanton–Moncada. Shelley and Maturin differ in that the former provides no omniscient narrator to guide our response, while the latter does offer "objective" commentary at some points. Both novels, however, project an image of a chaotic, incomprehensible universe. The theme is more obtrusive in *Melmoth,* but in *Frankenstein* Walton's turning back from his grand aim of unveiling the mysteries of the Arctic is a striking symbol of that incomprehensibility.

Shelley's novel is linked with *Melmoth* by Robert Hume in his essay on Negative Romanticism. Following Morse Peckham, Hume defines Negative Romanticism as "the outlook of those who have rebelled against static mechanism but not yet arrived at faith in organicism" (Hume, "Exuberant Gloom, Existential Agony, and Heroic Despair," 109). Faced with a "barren and alien world" in the absence of faith in the ordered universe of traditional religion, Negative Romanticism expresses, instead of hope, "bafflement, confusion, and despair," dealing with its discontents by "posing paradoxes, dwelling on the writer's pain." The prototype of the Negative Romantic myth is, of course, the Faust legend, in which "the protagonist is driven to evil, cannot or will not repent, and is destroyed." *Frankenstein* is a pure example of the basic form of this myth, encapsulated as "pain, No Exit, and damnation." *Melmoth,* according to Hume, elaborates the basic pattern by emphasizing "the grandeur of pain and endeavor" (Hume, 110, 111, 112, 126). These two novels, as we have already noted, share some obvious similarities—their focus on Faustian wanderers outcast from humanity, their common motif of fatal curiosity delving into "things man was not meant to know" (in the familiar horror-tale phrase), their frame stories and interpolated narratives.

Less obvious is the way young John in the frame of *Melmoth*, like Walton in the frame of *Frankenstein*, echoes the theme of fatal curiosity and presumption. Both are tempted to embrace the outcast wanderer's fate of alienation from human society and man's natural destiny. The root meaning of alienation—to make strange—has, as we have seen, a peculiar appositeness to the fantastic mode, whose effects characteristically arise from strangeness-in-familiarity. But in the early nineteenth century alienation was already being used in its modern sense, as estrangement, discord. The phenomenon, if not the word, is central to much Romantic poetry—for example, the Wordsworthian theme of self-consciousness as the cause of estrangement from nature. The "tragedy of self-awareness" and "excess of consciousness" are typical of the Romantic hero. He is "placed outside the structure of civilization," either by society's overt rejection of him or by an "introverted quality of mind" (Frye, 40, 41). Undeserved rejection certainly characterizes Frankenstein's monster, while Frankenstein, Walton, and John Melmoth all tend to isolate themselves by their self-conscious search for the "gnosis" that Frye describes as "a secret, perilous, and forbidden knowledge" (Frye, 106). John and Walton, warned by the tales unfolded to them, avoid the snare of alienation by turning back to the ordinary world of human affairs and forswearing the quest for things beyond humanity's natural limits.

The Faustian pattern and the theme of mortal overreaching suggest a religious background. S. L. Varnado associates Rudolf Otto's concept of the numinous with Gothic literature and makes a particular application to *Frankenstein*. Otto invented this word to identify the nonrational or suprarational element in religion (an element, we recall, that many eighteenth-century philosophers wished to eliminate). He associates the numinous "in its early stages," as Varnado points out, "with the preternatural" (Varnado, 12). One element not present, however, in the earliest concept of the holy is the ethical dimension, which emerges later, as rational theology develops. The sense of unworthiness associated with the holy originally had no necessary connection with law and its violation. Thus, though numinous as such is premoral, even before the numinous becomes linked to moral concepts of sin and duty, it has its own "value and disvalue." Varnado uses this aspect of the numinous to account for the way *Frankenstein* "projects a feeling of horror and evil that is disproportionate to the moral framework out of which Mary Shelley worked." Although Dr. Frankenstein (presumably like his creator) holds an Enlightenment scorn for doctrines of sin and guilt, he feels "the numinous disvalue attendant upon his profane experiments" (Varnado, 20). Though not precisely supernatural, the creation of the monster is preternatural—beyond nature—and thus entails a violation of deeply felt taboo. The absence of an omniscient (and authoritative) narrator leaves open the question of whether Frankenstein's aversion is an irrational atavism or evidence of a real disvalue built into the fabric of the universe. The 1817 preface, in fact, declines any authoritative role with the disclaimer: "The opinions which naturally spring from the character and situation of the hero are by no means to be conceived as existing always in my own conviction; nor is any inference justly to be drawn from the following pages as prejudicing any philosophical doctrine of whatever kind" (Shelley, 2). Joel Porte also reads *Frankenstein* in religious terms, characterizing the hero as a "guilt-ridden sinner-God whose damnable career involves, not benefaction, but death and destruction" (Porte, "In the Hands of an Angry God," 55). Frankenstein's presumptuous attempt to be as God is obvious, of course, not only in the subtitle, "The Modern Prometheus," but also in the monster's characterization of him as a negligent deity. Yet the doctor's intentions, as we know, are originally noble (or so he claims). The intertwinings and ambiguities of good and evil permeate his story; in *Frankenstein* the discourse of the fantastic is employed to cast doubt not so much on the ontological status of events as on their moral status.

As the reader will recall, *Frankenstein* begins with the letters of Robert Walton, Arctic explorer, to his sister. Walton confides to her his vision of the polar territory as "the region of beauty and delight, . . . a land surpassing in wonders and in beauty every region hitherto discovered on the habitable globe" (*Frankenstein,* 3–4). All he lacks is a friend of like temperament with whom to share his triumphs and ambitions; his aspirations set him apart from his peers and even estrange him from his ship's crew. In Frankenstein, ironically, he finds a kindred spirit who exerts the greatest efforts to dissuade him from his voyage. (Frankenstein's later apparent change of heart, when he castigates the ship's crew for wishing to turn back, may stem from impulsive sympathy for Walton or his own desire to have Walton proceed northward to carry the quest for the monster.) Walton compares himself, ominously, to the Ancient Mariner, but vows to "kill no albatross," despite the "love for the marvellous, a belief in the marvellous . . . which hurries me out of the common pathways of men." He goes so far as to say, "One man's life or death were but a small price to pay for the acquirement of the knowledge which I sought; for the dominion I should acquire" (*Frankenstein,* 10, 17). In other words, like Frankenstein and the monster, Walton is isolated from human society. Nor is Walton's ambition free from an egoistic desire for fame and dominion. (And surely it is significant that his choice of a seagoing vocation, like Crusoe's, constitutes disobedience to a father's injunctions.) Already the motif of an evil seed dormant in good intentions is present. Walton seeks this dominion mainly, it is true, for the good of humanity, but so, in the beginning, does Frankenstein; the latter therefore tells his story to deflect Walton from a fatal course.

The body of the novel consists of Walton's transcription of Frankenstein's first-person narrative. Frankenstein is aware of the strangeness of his tale:

> Prepare to hear of occurrences which are usually deemed marvellous. Were we among the tamer scenes of nature, I might fear to encounter your unbelief, perhaps your ridicule; but many things will appear possible in these wild and mysterious regions which would provoke the laughter of those unacquainted with the ever-varied powers of nature. (*Frankenstein,* 19)

Notice the reference to the "powers of nature," implying that the "marvellous" lies on a continuum with the "natural." Walton in fact has no substantial doubt of the tale's truth. His "love for the marvellous" predisposes him to believe in strange phenomena; furthermore, he regards Frankenstein with an attitude not far from hero worship. Hardly a critical audience, Walton is not the ideal surrogate for the reader. His sister Margaret, as narratee, functions as the reader's representative, for Walton strives to convince her of Frankenstein's nobility and the factual truth of the strange events. As evidence for the former, Walton can only offer his subjective conviction that Margaret herself, although "fastidious," would "appreciate the extraordinary merits of this wonderful man" (*Frankenstein,* 18). As evidence for the story's factuality, Walton recounts his own meeting with the monster.

Whether the monster is good or evil is a question harder to settle. As a potentially noble nature spoiled by a combination of society's rejection and his own impulsive violence, he fits the profile of the Gothic villain-hero. At the end of his narrative Frankenstein insists that the creature's "soul is as hellish as his form, full of treachery and fiendlike malice" (*Frankenstein,* 226). These bitter words may be excused as a result of the harrowing experiences Frankenstein has suffered. But he speaks of the creature in terms almost as harsh from the beginning. In the moment of its animation, he sees it as a "miserable monster," a "demoniacal corpse," which he regards with "breathless horror and disgust" (*Frankenstein,* 51–52). When the creature tells Frankenstein his adventures, the doctor momentarily acknowledges "some justice in his argument" and sees him as "a creature of fine sensations" (*Frankenstein,* 154). These feelings, however, alternate with those of revulsion, and the doctor soon regrets his reluctant promise to construct a female monster. Again he views the creature as "a fiend whose unparalleled barbarity had desolated my heart" (*Frankenstein,* 176). He never really gives the monster's claim to desire companionship and sympathy a fair hearing.

Walton, too, upon meeting the monster, is "at first touched by the expressions of his misery," but he quickly hardens his heart with the memory of Frankenstein's sufferings. The monster himself seems to take a more balanced view. While bemoaning the injustice he has suffered, he also acknowledges, "But it is true that I am a wretch. I have murdered the lovely and the helpless" (*Frankenstein,* 239, 241).

The monster's autobiography is nevertheless a catalogue of the persecution humanity has inflicted on him. Felix, whose aged father (blind, and thus unaware of the creature's physical repulsiveness) he befriends, the peasant whose little daughter he rescues, young William Frankenstein, even his own creator—all who see him spurn him with horror.* M. A. Goldberg, tracing the way Miltonic allusions form structural links among the novel's three concentric narratives, holds that Shelley transmutes the Miltonic doctrine of good and evil into the Godwinian theory that "virtue is essentially social" (Goldberg, "Moral and Myth in Mrs. Shelley's *Frankenstein,*" 33). The common guilt of Walton, Frankenstein, and the monster centers in their isolation from human society. Like Frankenstein, Walton "discovers his error in assuming that knowledge is a higher good than love or sympathy, and that it can be independent of the fellow-feeling afforded by a compassionate society" (Goldberg, 33). The absence of this "fellow-feeling," we recall, is the monster's chief cause for complaint as well as his motive for demanding a female companion.

To the "sanguinary laws of man" (*Frankenstein,* 152) and the cruel rejection he suffers, the monster attributes the corruption of his originally benignant nature. Thus all humanity is implicated in his crimes, for he does not choose isolation but has it thrust upon him. This guilty involvement is emphasized in the death of William (who, though an innocent child, also reacts with revulsion and thus symbolically epitomizes the rejection that corrupts the creature) and the trial of the servant Justine for his murder. Frankenstein's fiancée, Elizabeth, accuses herself of William's murder, for she let him wear the miniature that supposedly provoked the crime. The imperfect legal system convicts Justine, despite her innocence, and, driven to despair, she swears to a perjured confession. The priest, she says, "threatened and menaced, until I almost began to think that I was the monster that he said I was" (*Frankenstein,* 86). The community, therefore, is guilty of Justine's death, and she, though not a murderess, is certainly a liar. Though innocent of the crime for which she dies, she shares the universal human guilt. When the

---

*As an accursed wanderer isolated from humanity, the monster is reflected not only in Frankenstein, but also in Walton, by his self-comparison to the Ancient Mariner. This character type also suggests Cain and the Wandering Jew, favorite Romantic figures. The monster, indeed, resembles the dark, outcast, solitary brother—Cain, Esau, Ishmael—whose closeness to untamed nature allows him to share that nature's ambiguous blend of good and evil (Frye, 30). The creature has this kind of dispossessed brother relationship with the "civilized" Frankenstein.

priest convinces her she is a "monster," he is almost right, though for a mistaken reason. Justine is not untainted by the Original Sin embodied in the embittered creature. Though in a lesser mode than Dr. Frankenstein, she, too, is the monster's double—although she shares with Elizabeth and little William (himself, though only a child, already stained with the intolerance that rejects the creature) the distinction of being one of the most nearly innocent people in the story. Frankenstein, of course, holds himself directly responsible for all the monster's deeds, referring to William and Justine as "the first hapless victims to my unhallowed arts" (*Frankenstein,* 89). (Note the nonrational term "unhallowed.") Had he assumed proper responsibility for his creature, these two deaths would have been averted. But why, upon receiving his father's letter about William's death, does Frankenstein instantly leap to the conclusion that the monster is the murderer? What general source of guilt underlies his specific guilt?

Joel Porte's thesis implies that the primary subject of Gothic fiction is Original Sin. This critic's application of the religious sublime to the Gothic novel focuses on religious *fear,* which, he holds, springs from a characteristically Protestant (especially Calvinist) background. The terror in these novels, he says, arises from an awareness of guilt and accompanies a dramatic representation of "the dark rites of sin, guilt, and damnation" (Porte, 45). (His exemplary text is *The Monk.*) Even after the traditional "religious mystery" is discredited, its emotional content remains attached to tales of terror (Porte, 43). Though *Frankenstein,* as Goldberg explains, is undergirded by Godwinian philosophy, it is also thematically unified by allusions to *Paradise Lost;* the religious mystery of Original Sin is not alien to this novel (nor to *Melmoth,* which is the work of a clergyman). By Original Sin I mean what any Englishman would have understood from the *Book of Common Prayer,* that condition "whereby man is very far gone from original righteousness and is of his own nature inclined to evil" (article IX), so that "works done before the grace of Christ . . . are not pleasant to God, forasmuch as they spring not of faith" (article XIII). Victor Frankenstein's lifework, for instance, is doomed from the start by the pride that, unknown to himself, motivates his solitary trespass into forbidden realms. The monster's depredations seem to embody a sort of generalized guilt—mistakenly fastened upon Justine, claimed as their own by Frankenstein and Elizabeth, ultimately involving the whole human community—whose irony is highlighted by the monster's account of its own original benevolence and by Frankenstein's ostensibly lofty motives. The doctor describes his purpose thus: "Life and death appeared to me ideal bounds, which I should first break through, and pour a torrent of light into our dark world. A new species would bless me as its creator and source; many happy and excellent natures would owe their being to me" (*Frankenstein,* 47) Just as a stream cannot rise higher than its source, so Frankenstein, tainted with Original Sin, cannot create the perfection he imagines. Frye describes the novel as "a retelling of the account of the origin of evil, in a world where the only creators that we can locate are human ones" (Frye, 45). The flaw in Frankenstein's ambition is evident from the egoism implicit in his hardly disinterested hunger for praise and fame ("would bless me") and from the way, even in his initial enthusiasm, he thinks of his labor as "filthy creation" and testifies that "often did my human nature turn with loathing from my occupation" (*Frankenstein*, 48). In Varnado's terms, Frankenstein intuitively recognizes the "numinous disvalue" of his project even though he consciously disregards any such irrational factors. Presumably a disbeliever in Original Sin and in the whole concept of natural bounds that mankind is forbidden to break through, he nevertheless reacts with automatic revulsion to his own forbidden activity. Though his consciously held philosophy would not justify this revulsion, he comes to recognize, he thinks, the objective ground of the feeling. In retrospect he realizes that his obsession was "certainly unlawful, that is to say, not befitting the human mind" (*Frankenstein*, 48). It is noteworthy that Frankenstein's researches seem to awaken him to the realm of numinous value. Though his narrative gives us no reason to suspect him of atheism, he is certainly a rationalist. He says of his early life, "I do not ever remember to have trembled at a tale of superstition, or to have feared the apparition of a spirit" (*Frankenstein*, 45). Here he differs from Walton, who, we recall, is fascinated with the "marvellous." And Frankenstein's scorn for superstition makes it all the more ironic that he looks to occultists, not legitimate scientists, for inspiration and guidance in his research. His early rationalism also aids the credibility of his narrative, since such a character would be unlikely either to fabricate a wild tale or succumb to self-delusion. Eventually Frankenstein's meddling with forbidden knowledge makes him aware of the supernatural realm he has previously disregarded. Amid the isolation and despair of his wanderings, haunted by a sense of being cursed, he nevertheless finally comes to believe that "a spirit of good followed and directed my steps" (*Frankenstein*, 220). The mediated nature of the narrative makes it impossible to tell whether this impression is a consoling delusion or corresponds to something in fact, but the remark does illustrate how preternatural evil, in this case, the guilt of arrogating to oneself the power of creation, can open a character's eyes to its opposite. Yet the reader cannot help doubting whether the powers of goodness lend their support to a hero who believes "the spirits of the dead hovered round and instigated me to toil and revenge" (*Frankenstein*, 224). Walton's uncritical acceptance of this embittered narrator as a wronged and thoroughly noble genius leaves ambiguous the permutations of Original Sin that entangle Frankenstein and the monster with each other and with the rest of human society. Nor does Shelley provide the reader with the perspective that a response from Walton's sister would give.

Wolfgang Iser (in connection with *Humphrey Clinker*) says of epistolary fiction, "Through the letter form, the reader is confronted directly with the characters, and since none of the addressees writes in return, the reader must take their place. The events are not coordinated for him" (Iser, *The Implied Reader,* 71). *Frankenstein* places this kind of demand on the reader. If Margaret is our surrogate, she is a silent one. Her brother thinks she would admire Frankenstein as he does, but his expectation is obviously biased. Her response might guide ours, but we must supply that response. The space she ought to occupy constitutes one of Iser's "gaps of indeterminacy" (Iser, 226). Though the varied judgments pronounced by Frankenstein, the monster, and Walton offer clues to resolving the indeterminacy, the discrepancies among them leave us without definitive guidance. Though better informed than Frankenstein's bewildered father or the authorities who convict Justine, we cannot wholly fill the gap.

Melmoth the Wanderer, in contrast, exhibits the constant presence of an omniscient narrator in numerous footnotes. Maturin, in fact, sometimes commits what certain critical schools would call wanton violation of the story's autonomy; for instance, Iser declares that too predictable a fulfillment of the reader's expectations, resulting in an excess of clarity, is tantamount to didacticism. Maturin glosses one of Melmoth's tirades thus:

> As, by a mode of criticism equally false and unjust, the worst sentiments of my worst characters... have been represented as *my own,* I must here trespass so far on the patience of the reader as to assure him, that the sentiments ascribed to the stranger are diametrically opposite to mine, and that I have purposely put them into the mouth of an agent of the enemy of mankind. (*Melmoth,* 233)

This passage places the implied reader solidly on the narrator's side against Melmoth. It is assumed that we too find Melmoth's remarks reprehensible and need to be reassured that the narrator concurs with our sentiments. (Peavoy attributes pronouncements like this, however, to Maturin's "unwillingness to accept his own story's implications" [Peavoy, 267]. I prefer not to speculate on the author's psychological state.)

While the omniscient voice's pressure on the reader is not usually so blatant, the direction in which we are being guided is clear. Melmoth is an agent, almost an incarnation, of the enemy of mankind. Within the mediated narratives, however, Melmoth's moral status is more problematic. Even that phrase, "the enemy of mankind," takes on an ambiguous significance. Though Maturin's preface attributes the concept of the novel to one of his own sermons, thus preparing the reader for a didactic exemplum, in practice the story's theme is less clear-cut than this model would suggest.

The nested boxes of mediated narratives offer the reader an opportunity to reject the attitude of the omniscient narrator (who is met in the opening and closing sections and in the footnotes). Within the interpolated stories we are invited to experience a gradually growing sympathy for Melmoth. This sympathy is engendered by the accumulating evidence that Melmoth's crimes are slight compared to those of many mortals. The Wanderer's sardonic descriptions of human society in the "Tale of the Indians" suggest, in fact, the disillusionment of an initially noble nature—if an avatar of Satan, then of Satan in the early books of *Paradise Lost*. Melmoth, like Frankenstein's monster, though he may be evil, claims to be far less so than the rest of the world. All mankind is implicated in this evil; Melmoth, too, highlights the pervasive existence of Original Sin. David Eggenschwiler discovers a number of related themes in *Melmoth*—isolation, imprisonment, broken family ties, obsession, excess, the craving for power, and the violation of the bounds of nature. He encapsulates the topics of "restless consciousness, the insufficiency of life's banquet, the tales of the invisible world," as the novel's unifying motifs (Eggenschwiler, 179). To this list we may add persecution, the perversion of religious love, and the dangers of "apathy within the self," as discussed by Jack Null in "Structure and Theme in *Melmoth the Wanderer*" (Null, 147). All these motifs may be subsumed, as Null hints, under the umbrella of a quest for the true enemy of mankind. I see the novel's central theme to be the source and nature of evil. While the omniscient narrator (in his footnotes, for example) applies this satanic label—enemy of mankind—to Melmoth, the narrative structure creates ambiguities that preclude unqualified acceptance of such a simple evaluation. The true enemy must still be sought.

Null sees the novel's disjointed structure as reflecting "the disorientation caused by the characters' loss of values" in "a world become madhouse in which the characters search, aimlessly and unsuccessfully, for selfhood, sanity, salvation" (Null, 137). While this view of the structure is unquestionably fruitful, I hold that the fragmented, mediated narratives have the additional function of rendering problematic the omniscient narrator's straightforward equation of Melmoth with evil. The entanglements between frame and interpolated tales, and among the various tales, illustrate how evil, Original Sin, is deeply rooted in all human beings; to single out Melmoth's sin as uniquely heinous is ultimately hypocritical. The characters are indeed engaged in a quest, not the least young John Melmoth, the reader's representative within the novel. John's miserly uncle, from whom the young man inherits the headship of the family, is secretly obsessed with Melmoth and associated with him by his own probable damnation. John, whose very name is identical to the mysterious ancestor's, inherits the obsession along with the property. John suffers from a "feverish curse of curiosity which was consuming his inmost soul" (*Melmoth*, 44). Melmoth himself tells John that the young man is "fortified by that vain and desperate inquisitiveness, which might, at a former period, have made you my victim" (*Melmoth*, 408). John's quest for knowledge of his ancestor is duplicated in the life of Stanton, the first tale John discovers. After his unjustified confinement for madness, Stanton pursues Melmoth with more avidity than before, with a single-mindedness that he admits to be "a species of insanity," the "master-passion" but also "the master-torment of his life" (*Melmoth*, 44). In his search for Melmoth, Stanton also becomes a kind of Faustian wanderer, as Frankenstein does in hunting the monster.

The fragmented nature of the Stanton manuscript foregrounds the importance of documents themselves and the difficulty of attaining certainty about either facts or values. John's perusal of the manuscript becomes a kind of archaeology. He is compared to an "antiquarian, unfolding with trembling hand the calcined leaves of an Herculaneum manuscript, and hoping to discover some lost line of the Aeneis in Virgil's own autograph" (*Melmoth*, 44). Stanton's memoir is "discoloured, obliterated, and mutilated beyond any that had ever before exercised the patience of a reader" (*Melmoth*, 21). How the document was written, delivered to the Melmoth family, and preserved is carefully explained, as is the history of each of the manuscripts featured in the novel. Though the Spaniard Moncada's verbatim memory of all the interpolated tales within his story demands the acceptance of a highly artificial convention, the way each narrative comes to be recorded or recited is accounted for plausibly enough.

The plausibility of the story as a whole is enhanced by the realism of presentation employed throughout, notably in the first few chapters. Like many nineteenth-century Gothic novels, *Melmoth* begins with action and setting that could be found in any realistic novel. Young John's family difficulties and college experiences, the gritty penury of his uncle's household (illustrated by hard physical details), the opportunistic behavior of the servants, and the touches of Irish folklore and dialect contribute to the immediacy of the opening incidents. John is the reader's contemporary (his uncle's death is dated in 1816) and, like the implied reader, takes a skeptical attitude toward the supernatural. The novel's first intimation of the nonrational concerns the local wise-woman, healer, and "Sybil" who supports herself "by practising on the fears, the ignorance, and the sufferings of beings as miserable as herself" (*Melmoth*, 7). John's distrust of this creature indicates that he shares the skepticism implied by the narrator's ironic catalogue of her powers. As a recognizably contemporary protagonist, John carries a rationalistic mind-set like the reader's into a social environment inclined to credulity but by no means blindly superstitious (e.g., the servants attribute old Melmoth's ravings about the Devil to sickness, not literal haunting). Protagonist and reader, together confronting the gradually revealed facts about Melmoth the Wanderer, move together from doubt to acceptance of these facts.

At first John is not predisposed to believe in Stanton's adventures. The glimpse of Melmoth at the miser's bedside is not enough to make John credit his uncle's claim that the Wanderer still lives. The young heir rationalizes the incident and, midway through the Stanton manuscript, still confronts the tale in a mood "perplexed and unsatisfied, not knowing what connexion this Spanish story could have with his ancestor" (*Melmoth,* 29). Yet his curiosity drives him on to complete the reading of the cryptic, half-legible document. His next encounter with the Wanderer partakes of the fantastic, for he cannot decide whether it is "in a dream or not, that he saw the figure of his ancestor at the door" (*Melmoth,* 45). Upon waking, however, he finds material evidence in the form of the mark of Melmoth's grip on his wrist. From this point the reader, and probably John as well, is predisposed to credit Moncada's tale. The surface mystery of the novel shifts from whether Melmoth's diabolical immortality really exists to how he gained that immortality. This secret is not revealed until the penultimate chapter. By that chapter, when Moncada's narrative is, not completed, but suspended just short of completion, John has moved so far toward belief in the supernatural that he conceives "the wild hope of seeing the original of that portrait he had destroyed, burst from the walls and take up the fearful tale himself" (*Melmoth,* 406). Though John and Moncada are properly horrified, they are not particularly surprised when the Wanderer does appear at the precisely appropriate moment to gather up the interlaced strands of the tale. A kind of fate beyond coincidence operates (like the coincidence of two friends who come together and find they have been playing roles in the same drama, in *Horrid Mysteries* and *The Necromancer*), the same fate that shipwrecks Moncada on the Melmoth estate and no other. Moncada himself alludes to this fatality with the assurance that "we are all beads strung on the same string . . . our union is indissoluble" (*Melmoth,* 229). Typical not only of Gothic fiction but of romance in general, this "union," transcending causality as ordinarily understood, is the novel's most strikingly supernatural feature aside from the character of Melmoth himself.

If such fatality does operate, the nature of reality is quite different from our usual assumptions about it. An undercurrent of questioning about reality and illusion, natural and supernatural, runs through *Melmoth,* though not as pervasively as the problem of evil. As already mentioned, the fragmented condition of Stanton's memoir suggests the fundamental incomprehensibility of the universe. We continually encounter gaps that must be filled by conjecture. Moncada's adventures draw attention to the question of whether supernatural phenomena exist. Like many a Gothic hero and heroine, Moncada is subjected to a simulated haunting. His persecution, however, strikes deeper than most of the spectral hoaxes in this kind of fiction. Moncada's suffering is explicitly a horror of the soul. His gradually solidifying certainty that the satanic attacks are fraudulent does nothing to alleviate his despair. The emotion produced by a supernatural experience can be independent of its objective reality, in situations of soul-freezing horror as well as those of soul-expanding Radcliffean terror: "When art assumes the omnipotence of reality, when we feel we suffer as much from an illusion as from truth, our sufferings lose all dignity and all consolation" (*Melmoth,* 122).

Can it be that the monks who choreograph Moncada's ordeal are, chillingly, analogues of the author, like the omnipotent conspiracy in Don Carlos' memoirs? When reality and illusion become indistinguishable in their effects, Moncada finds himself manipulated and his suffering trivialized, as does the protagonist of *Horrid Mysteries.* Is the omniscient narrator himself trustworthy, if he is to be identified with the implied author, and the author's activity can be represented by this kind of psychological torture? Though Moncada attempts prayer, the prevailing emotion conveyed by his story is despair at confronting a senseless, hostile universe. As Peavoy says of the Stanton episode, "the narrator seems to join . . . Melmoth in mocking man's efforts to find or create order" (Peavoy, 240). In such a disordered universe isolation includes the inability to share any certainty one may acquire. The central hiatus in Stanton's manuscript covers the terms of Melmoth's temptation. Throughout the novel, whenever the Wanderer reveals his diabolical secret, there is a break in the narrative. Moncada calls the secret "that incommunicable condition which I am forbid to reveal" (*Melmoth,* 183). The truth about Melmoth's bargain seems to represent the arcana of the universe, largely unknowable, and once fathomed, unspeakable (like the incommunicable secret of Frankenstein's exact techique for animating dead flesh).

The idea of the incommunicable is embodied in the varying reliability of the interlaced narratives. The first source of information available to John is village folklore. He hears the family legend from his uncle's housekeeper and the local folk-healer. The gossip of servants mutters through the opening section, as they constantly "whispered their fearful suggestions to each other" (*Melmoth,* 46). Oral tradition preserves the legend of the Wanderer in its own fluid manner, predating the written accounts of systematic researchers. Melmoth's "life is doomed to be recorded in incredible legends that moulder in the libraries of the curious, and to be disbelieved and scorned even by those who exhaust sums on their collection"; though still alive, he "has become already the subject of written memoirs, and the theme of traditional history" (*Melmoth,* 304). These remarks, by a collector of such legends, cast a shadow of uncertainty on all the stories that make up the novel. A reminder of their status as tales, and therefore of problematic authenticity, appears in Moncada's comment to John, "Romances have made your country, Sir, familiar with tales of subterranean passages, and supernatural horrors" (*Melmoth,* 148). This metatextual statement emphasizes the mental horrors that Moncada, in just such a typical Gothic situation, inflicts on himself. Though his images of all the supernatural horrors "that the interminable passages, the livid light, and the diabolical companion, might suggest" turn out to be illusory, the emotions experienced are genuine (*Melmoth,* 149). Delusion and deception haunt Moncada throughout his story; he must evaluate the sincerity of the brother who suddenly converts from enmity to fraternal devotion, the patricidal monk who ostensibly helps him escape from the convent, and the Jews who shelter him. Of the three, the monk alone turns out to be fundamentally treacherous; after repeated questions and assurances concerning his reliability, at the last moment he delivers up Moncada for recapture.

Within the novel there is only one completely knowledgeable source of information, other than the omniscient narrator—Melmoth himself. Can his version of events, however, be fully trusted? Although an informed narrator, Melmoth may not be a reliable one. He may be either deceptive or self-deceived. The first extended narrative recounted by the Wanderer is "The Lovers' Tale," within the story of Immalee/Isidora. Melmoth tells this tale to Don Francisco, Isidora's father, supposedly to warn the old man of his daughter's impending fate. Francisco has just heard the story of Guzman's family narrated by the folklorist collecting legends of Melmoth—another analogue of John and Stanton, but the merchant proves to be an inattentive audience. He only half-hears the incredible story, barely notices the detail of the Wanderer's temptation, and does not remember it accurately when drawn to his attention. In short, he has no idea that the events related belong to his own story. With a kind of commonsensical obtuseness, he considers the "Lovers' Tale" equally irrelevant to his experience. He dismisses the Melmoth legends as "tales that have no more application to me than the legend of the Cid, and may be as apocryphal as the ballad of Roncesvalles" (*Melmoth*, 382). The reader knows that, ironically, the wildest extravagances of romance are in fact central to the vital concerns of this humdrum merchant. To make the point inescapably plain, Melmoth tells Don Francisco his own story, under the anonymous designation of "a certain Spanish merchant." Melmoth claims to issue his warning for "the safety of a being of more value than all your race beside," i.e., Isidora (*Melmoth*, 382, 339). The Wanderer's concern seems sincere, for otherwise why would he jeopardize the success of his seduction by giving a warning at all? But on the other hand, if he really cares for Isidora, why does he not simply renounce her instead of relying on her unimaginative father's response to a cryptic message? Has the Devil put Melmoth under some compulsion that forces him to pursue his victim against his own will? His deepest motives at this juncture remain a mystery. In his final encounter with Moncada and John, Melmoth reveals the condition of his diabolical immortality—or, rather, he seems to reveal it. The sentences of his confession begin, "It has been reported of me," "It has been said," and "If this be true." We tend to believe his statement that "no one has ever exchanged destinies with Melmoth the Wanderer" (*Melmoth*, 408–9), but room for doubt remains. The author wisely bars us from Melmoth's innermost thoughts. Even in "The Wanderer's Dream," we are presented with his actions and sensations, not his emotions. The precise extent of his evil and of the good that may cling to him remains problematic. The omniscient narrator's disclaimer (quoted above) of any sympathy between Melmoth's views and his own throws responsibility for evaluating Melmoth's character upon the reader.

As readers attempting to fill the "gap of indeterminacy," we cannot find reliable guidance in identifying with any particular narratee. Moncada's narratee is young John, who, though admirable enough in his concern for the victims of the storm, is disqualified as a model for our response by his feverish desire to unearth Melmoth's secret. Moncada himself serves as narratee for several interpolated tales (such as the patricidal monk's confession and the Immalee manuscript), but the doubt and despair generated by his isolation warn us against completely identifying with him. Immalee is the audience for Melmoth's most extensive self-disclosure, but she too, is not a fully adequate surrogate for the reader; though superior to the implied reader in purity of soul, she is inferior in knowledge of the world. Her father, another of Melmoth's narratees, is the least adequate of all the response models presented for our consideration. Except for the omniscient author's occasional intrusion by way of footnotes, our implied prescription for reacting to the nested narratives is essentially negative; the less than adequate responses of the various narratees show us modes of interpretation to avoid. The empty space between these limited responses (in Iser's terms) is the gap we must attempt to fill with the proper interpretation.

Questions of the Wanderer's character, the degree of truth in his legend, the reliability of various kinds of narrative, and the nature of reality come to a focus on the problem of the objective reality of good and evil. The patricidal monk who pretends to aid and then betrays Moncada holds good and evil to be delusions. When he says, "I laugh at human passions and human cares,— vice and virtue, religion and impiety; they are all the result of petty localities, and artificial situation" (*Melmoth,* 165), he resembles the egoistic heroes of the Marquis de Sade. As evidence for his philosophy, the monk offers a tale of two lovers, imprisoned in a convent cell, reduced to attempted cannibalism. Their behavior, he claims, demonstrates that the genuine human motivation is nothing more than the animal instinct of self-preservation. This monk, however, proves to be a sadistic traitor and murderer; might his tale not be a fabrication for the pleasure of terrrifying Moncada? Even Melmoth does not consign all of humanity to such depths; he recognizes the goodness of Isidora. He also admits the remote possibility that Don Francisco may put his daughter's welfare above his own. For the most part, though, Melmoth views the human species cynically, as his satiric speeches to Isidora show. He points out that even Don Francisco, "an orthodox and inveterate Catholic," who "must abhor the enemy of mankind," has "often acted as his agent" (*Melmoth,* 333). Upon Don Francisco's outrage at being called an agent of the Devil, Melmoth counters with a catalogue of the secret sins of which every man is sometimes guilty. Sin permeates the human condition, and every person, though less flamboyantly than Melmoth, is equally an agent of evil. The

Wanderer demands, "What enemy has man so deadly as himself?" (*Melmoth*, 334).

Is Melmoth the voice of truth on this subject? The ubiquity of corruption seems borne out by all the narratives. Even Moncada, whose tale presents him as a bewildered, persecuted innocent (like Sade's Justine, attracting evil by his very inoffensiveness), confesses to falling into hypocrisy and duplicity. He appears different only in degree from the monk who professes "the theology of utter hostility to all beings whose sufferings may mitigate mine. In this flattering theory, your crimes become my virtues" (*Melmoth*, 174). The narrator of Isidora's tale provides a corrective to Melmoth's view of humanity by contrasting Isidora's emotional intensity with "the stony apathy of one who had traversed life from Dan to Beersheba, and found all barren, or—made it so" (*Melmoth*, 391). (The verbal echo of Judges 20:1 reinforces, perhaps, our awareness that Melmoth stands under divine condemnation and therefore cannot be trusted.) The Wanderer's judgment of humanity, then, may be a delusion of his own. And Isidora's purity presents at least one exception to the supposed universality of evil; her goodness, we are to suppose, touches the heart of the Wanderer himself, revealing remnants of humanity. This goodness, though, comes to fruition on a desert island. Is isolation from human society the only condition in which virtue can flourish? Or is the compassion of John Melmoth's retainers, exerting themselves to rescue the victims of shipwreck, a reliable index to human nature rather than a rare exception? No definitive answer is provided.

Eggenschwiler says that the "ethical and religious norm of the natural" implied in Immalee/Isidora's tropical idyll is finally shown to be "not fully human," for "man's desire for the unnatural was a symptom of his spirituality, and . . . man's demonic drives were closely related to his striving for salvation." Isidora's growth, according to this critic, is a sign, like the dark obsessions of the other characters, "that man is a spiritual being who cannot live entirely in the natural world" (Eggenschwiler, 166, 177). Melmoth himself declares that his own existence is, in effect, a proof of God's:

> Infidel and scoffer as I may appear to you, there is no martyr of the Christian church, who in other times blazed for his God, that has borne or exhibited a more resplendent illustration of his faith, than I shall bear one day—and for ever. . . . I am doomed to bear my attestation to the truth of the gospel, amid fires that shall burn for ever and ever. (*Melmoth*, 298–99)

Along the same line, it is suggestive that the phantom music heralding Melmoth's appearance to his victims consists of "celestial sounds, that seem to prepare us for heaven," though they actually "announce the presence of an incarnate fiend" (*Melmoth*, 33). The ambiguity of the Wanderer's character embodies the indissoluble union of good and evil in a fallen world. Following Eggenschwiler, we might say that Maturin's novel illustrates how (in cases like Isidora's) experience of the supernatural, even in its darker aspect, can awaken the mind to spiritual values.

At the end of his life the Wanderer attempts to absolve himself from some degree of the evil attributed to him: "If all that fear has invented, and credulity believed of me be true, to what does it amount? That if my crimes have exceeded those of mortality, so will my punishment. I have been on earth a terror, but not an evil to its inhabitants. None can participate in my destiny but with his own consent." (*Melmoth,* 408). Once again Melmoth proves himself not completely reliable; he has brought disaster upon the innocent at least once, in the deaths of the bride and bridegroom whose funeral Stanton witnessed. However, his main point is clear: The Devil or his agent cannot claim a victim without the cooperation of the evil principle rooted in the individual's own will. Those who encounter Melmoth may, like John Melmoth and Stanton, be implicated in the quest for forbidden knowledge, but may also, like Isidora, rise through acquaintance with evil and suffering to an apprehension of the Divine.

In both *Melmoth* and *Frankenstein* we have seen contemporary characters—John and Walton—drawn into networks of incredible events, which promise a lifting of the veil between ordinary life and the preternatural or supernatural realm. The reader, assumed to be initially skeptical, is induced to step beyond this veil by the presence of a character he can identify with and also by the realistic techniques with which the strange events are presented. At the same time, in a manner typical of the fantastic mode, the very ordinariness of the character and vividness of detail contribute to the disorienting effect of the extraordinary events. Both novels exhibit spatial and temporal distancing techniques, as well as temporal dislocation of plot from story, which we have identified as typical of fantastic fiction. Multiple narrators foreground the issues of the nature of evidence and the reliability of witnesses, and in Maturin's novel, in particular, the problem of testimony is exacerbated by the presence of narrators accused of madness or crime (Stanton and Moncada). While *Horrid Mysteries* centers on an isolated, alienated protagonist, *Frankenstein* and *Melmoth* present a plethora of isolated characters, some suffering persecution, others choosing their own isolation. The resulting atmosphere of alienation finds an objective correlative in the motif of the incommunicable secret; in contrast to the secrets in Radcliffe's romances (e.g., Emily's black veil and Ellena's parentage), whose solutions are usually anticlimactic, the secrets in these two novels partake more fully of the "occult."

We next turn to treatments of the quest for the secret behind the veil that, in their attempt to marry science and the occult, have affinities with *Frankenstein.* In J. S. Le Fanu's Dr. Hesselius, intent on taming the inexplicable by asserting a rational principle where one may not exist, we meet a descendant of Dr. Frankenstein. Lytton's Margrave, like Frankenstein, pursues forbidden knowledge and, like Melmoth, roams the world cloaked in unnatural immortality. Both Le Fanu and Lytton use the discourse of the fantastic to explore the ontological status of the supernatural.

Edward Bulwer-Lytton

5

Science and the Supernatural in Two Victorian Fantasists

We now take up several stories that hesitate between supernatural and preternatural world views. Mundane explanations for weird events are entertained, in the form of disease, delusion, or hoax, but the central concern is usually to distinguish the supernatural from the occult (that which is hidden from the ordinary observer but clear to the specialist). Granted that events that would popularly be called supernatural have occurred, can they be explained in scientific rather than superstitious terms? Though the theme of supernatural reality in the highest sense is present in several of these stories, it coexists uneasily with the attempt to ascribe strange events to obscure but comprehensible causes.

Why does this endeavor seem to preoccupy Victorian fantasists? It is now a commonplace (replacing the old assumptions about the "complacent" nineteenth century) that this age was one of doubt and confusion, in which "the traditional framework of thought was breaking down" and intellectuals were conscious of facing alternatives in belief (Houghton, *The Victorian Frame of Mind 1830–1870,* 8). Throughout the period we encounter "the fear or suspicion, or simply the vague uneasy feeling, that one was not sure he believed what he believed" (Houghton, 21). Rapid advances in knowledge bore considerable responsibility for this state of mind. Every new discovery or theory (especially evolution, which we shall find to be a particular concern of Edward Bulwer-Lytton's) threatened to supplant the Christian world view with "the scientific picture of a vast mechanism of cause and effect, acting by physical laws that governed even man himself" (Houghton, 68). This suspension between views of the nature of the universe finds a fitting counterpart in the fantastic mode, wherein the mind is suspended between two (or three) theories of the supernatural. It is not surprising that authors of supernatural fantasy try to affirm the existence of man's spiritual part while accommodating rather than ignoring contemporary scientific thought. Can the two points of view be credibly combined? (As we shall see in the next chapter, *Dracula* makes an especially ambitious attempt at this combination.)

Irish mystery and ghost-story writer Joseph Sheridan Le Fanu, in the stories under discussion, leaves the question unresolved, for in the absence of an omniscient narrator the exact nature of his supernatural entities is not defined. In each case—the stories are presented precisely as "cases"— conflicting perspectives on events fall short of prescribing a response for the reader, who seems invited to consider the nature of reality a problem lacking any definitive solution. Lytton—who is best known for his historical fiction, particularly *The Last Days of Pompeii*—presents himself in familiar Gothic style as editor of his romance, providing guidance for his reader and avowedly offering evidence that in the contemporary science-oriented world a spiritual view of the universe is still valid.

This chapter concerns Lytton's *A Strange Story* (1862) and three tales from Le Fanu's *In a Glass Darkly* (1886). I reserve Lytton's novel for last because of its great length and because it anticipates the subject of the final chapter. All three of the Le Fanu stories, "Green Tea," "The Familiar," and "Carmilla," are framed by their supposed source in the casebooks of one Dr. Martin Hesselius.* I treat these three stories together because they share the character of Hesselius and the narrative doubt attending him, even though only "Carmilla," strictly speaking, fits within my stated boundaries for Gothic fiction—as defined by the haunted edifice and the Gothic villain-hero. "Carmilla" alone enjoys the benefit of a typical Gothic setting, an ancestral castle in Styria. We could, however (as we shall see), make a case for Hesselius as an overreacher like Frankenstein, obsessed with the impious project of reducing the supernatural to the natural (as Frankenstein tries to comprehend the spark of life in merely material terms). Like *A Strange Story,* the three tales employ first-person and mediated narration. Le Fanu and Lytton both use these techniques to foreground problems of conflicting testimony and the difficulty of distinguishing between fact and fantasy. Both focus on alienated characters. The haunted figures in "Green Tea" and "The Familiar" are isolated, by the persecution they suffer, from their skeptical contemporaries, as is Lytton's protagonist. All these characters' isolation is exacerbated by contrast with the commonplace world they inhabit. The heroine of "Carmilla," dwelling in her ancestral castle, is an exception, but she labors to present her family as ordinary, remarking on their income and the economy of their life-style, even making a point of their part-English heritage. All the stories discussed take advantage of temporal distance, setting the main action in a personal, rather than historical, past. "Carmilla" and the last part of *A Strange Story* use spatial distancing (exotic settings) as well. Le Fanu's tales are also comparable to Lytton's novel in that *A Strange Story* also features what we may call the "occult doctor" motif. This figure, who reaches his

---

*I quote from all three of these stories as reprinted in *Best Ghost Stories of J. S. Le Fanu,* ed. E. F. Bleiler.

culmination in Bram Stoker's Van Helsing, embodies the attempt to harmonize the supernatural with the nineteenth century's advances in scientific knowledge.

Hesselius' cases are introduced by an unnamed editor, Hesselius' medical secretary for twenty years. This younger man (thirty-five years Hesselius' junior) has been "carefully educated in medicine and surgery," though he has never practiced ("Green Tea," 178). This training presumably qualifies the editor to judge the validity of Hesselius' diagnoses. On the other side of the question of judgment, however, we cannot help noticing the editor's strong bias in Hesselius' favor: "In Dr. Martin Hesselius, I found my master. His knowledge was immense, his grasp of a case was an intuition. He was the very man to inspire a young enthusiast, like me, with awe and delight. My admiration has stood the test of time and survived the separation of death. I am sure it was well-founded" ("Green Tea," 178). That last sentence might waken a reader's suspicion; why is it necessary to make the statement at all? The editor's self-characterization as an enthusiast admits that he is impressionable, as is consistent with his impaired state of health (a result of the accident that barred him from the medical profession). Hence there may be a question of the editor's ability to pass a fair judgment on Dr. Hesselius. His admiration, even awe, for his "master" warns us not to expect objectivity. In presenting a narrative taken from Hesselius' letters to a professor of chemistry, he calls himself a "faithful, though . . . by no means a graceful translator" from the original French and German ("Green Tea," 179). Yet in the same sentence he admits having altered the style in minor ways, changed names, and omitted or shortened some passages. He has also, the reader discovers, removed most of the epistolary markers from the letters. In short, he paraphrases rather than translates. (One reason for his alterations, of course, is that his implied reader is a layman who would not grasp Hesselius' medical technicalities.) The story is further distanced from the original events by an intervening time span of sixty-four years. The separation of death reminds us that the editor has no recent experience of Hesselius to bridle his awe; there has been ample time and opportunity for idealization.

The documentary structure of the tale functions in two contradictory ways: The editor's meticulous account of his sources and how he treats them is meant to authenticate the facts. The more circumstantial the background of the story, the more credible it is. But the documents validate the events in this way mainly for the implied reader *within* the fiction, the reader in Le Fanu's secondary world who is seeking knowledge of a real-life Hesselius. For a reader in the primary world (i.e., the universe "real" to us) on the other hand, the nested system of narrators draws attention to the number of voices through which the story is filtered before it reaches us. Unlike an omniscient narrator, a narrator who is also a character can err or lie (as Todorov points out [*The Fantastic*, 83]).

The doctor's reliability as a narrator is put into question in several ways. His self-confidence, though justified according to the editor's enthusiastic evaluation, is apt to impress the reader as arrogance. After his first meeting with Jennings, the victim of the haunting, Hesselius mystifies his hostess with a series of leading questions that imply inexplicable knowledge of Jennings' background. This Sherlock-Holmes-like performance, presumably based on acute observation, is not even explained to the reader (unlike Holmes' deductions, whose rationale is always revealed in the end). Hesselius claims to have treated 57 cases like Jennings' without a single failure, a claim unsupported by other testimony. The editor, we might assume, would correct this statement if necessary, except that we have already noticed his hero worship of the doctor. Hesselius rationalizes his failure to cure Jennings by pointing out that he had not yet begun to treat the unfortunate man. He further dissociates himself from Jennings' case by attributing the victim's self-destruction, not to the haunting, but to "hereditary suicidal mania" ("Green Tea," 207). No grounds for this diagnosis are offered, though it is foreshadowed by the mention of Jennings' "silent and moping" father, given to seeing ghosts ("Green Tea," 184). As Jack Sullivan (to whose chapters on Le Fanu I am heavily indebted) says, Hesselius' primary motive seems to be a "determination to validate his theories" (Sullivan, *Elegant Nightmares*, 28).

An unpleasant desire to discredit Jennings appears in the conclusion of Hesselius' narrative. During the victim's lifetime Hesselius continually refers to him as "my friend" ("Green Tea," 187 and passim), but after his death by suicide Hesselius seems to distance himself. Upon meeting a servant with hands stained by Jennings' blood, in fact, the doctor significantly says, "I drew back a little." Hesselius' literal drawing back from the sight of blood suggests a figurative withdrawal from his relationship with the deceased. In the concluding section the late friend becomes "poor Mr. Jennings" ("Green Tea," 203, 207). Immediately after the suicide Hesselius says, "I feel like a man who has but half waked from a frightful and monotonous dream. My memory rejects the picture with incredulity and horror." Yet on the very next page he trivializes the experience (perhaps as a defense mechanism) with the assertion, "There is no one affliction of mortality more easily and certainly reducible, with a little patience, and a rational confidence in the physician." Hesselius' information about the creature haunting the Rev. Jennings is derived, of course, entirely from Jennings himself; even the doctor's knowledge of the putative suicide is second-hand, from the servant's report. We have, therefore, no basis for denying Hesselius' claim that the victim "had not yet given me . . . his full and unreserved confidence" ("Green Tea," 205, 206, 207). In effect, Jennings' fate is his own fault; the doctor is exonerated and his reputation undiminished.

Uncertainty about the reliability of the narrators (Hesselius and Jennings) adumbrates the uncertainty about the source of Jennings' affliction.

In what sense is the haunting supernatural? The clergyman suffers from the apparition of a black monkey with glowing eyes, which torments him with obscene and blasphemous suggestions, especially in the pulpit and at his prayers. At first Jennings tries to explain his affliction to himself as "purely disease, a well-known physical affection [*sic*], as distinctly as small-pox or neuralgia" ("Green Tea," 195). But at the moment of formulating this naturalistic argument he disbelieves it; to him the monkey is a messenger from hell. The Latin work by Swedenborg (the "Arcana Caelestia") that he consults confirms this view. "When man's interior sight is opened . . . there appear the things of another life," writes the mystic, and adds, "There are with every man at least two evil spirits" ("Green Tea," 186).

Hesselius makes no direct comment on this theory but probably does not concur with it. He holds that Jennings' interior sight has indeed been opened to allow him to see spirits, but Hesselius' theory of the spirit world differs from the orthodox one. He teaches "that the essential man is a spirit, that the spirit is an organised substance" comparable to "light or electricity." His "Metaphysical Medicine" accepts as real phenomena traditionally supposed supernatural, while supplanting the traditional explanation of these phenomena with scientific theory ("Green Tea," 181, 182). Communication between human and nonhuman intelligences is caused by disturbances of a fluid originating in the brain and circulating, like blood, through the nerves. Hesselius makes the curious assertion that "the nature of that fluid is spiritual, though not immaterial" ("Green Tea," 206). Spirit, contrary to orthodox belief, becomes simply a rarefied state of matter. This mechanistic model of the soul clashes, the reader may suppose, with Hesselius' frequent references to God's care. If the soul (so-called) can be assigned a physical rather than a spiritual origin, God might seem almost superfluous. The doctor reassures Jennings, "You are in His hands and in the power of no other being," yet his usual prescription for such afflictions is "the simple application of iced eau-de-cologne" ("Green Tea," 201, 207). Again alongside Jennings' spiritual agony and despair, Hesselius' explanations and recommendations appear reductive and trivializing.

Jennings' suffering, indeed, is underdetermined. According to Hesselius, the haunting springs simply from the effect on the nervous fluid of too much green tea. (The understatement of the title, as Sullivan remarks [Sullivan, 18], conveys an irony verging on the absurdist.) This explanation does not, in the final analysis, mend matters, since even if human beings are protected from seeing them, malignant spirits like the "monkey" still exist. Jennings has been writing a book on pagan religion, which he discovers to be dangerous to the Christian mind—"the subject is a degrading fascination and the Nemesis sure" ("Green Tea," 192). The clergyman obviously feels guilt for indulging in this research, but Hesselius does not even mention this possible "cause" in his diagnosis. Whether green tea or unhallowed study, the cause seems incommensurate with the result. Through the ambiguities of this story, Le Fanu offers a glimpse of a universe like H. P. Lovecraft's, in which preternatural horrors strike ordinary people almost at random. Le Fanu's clergyman resembles a Lovecraftian antiquarian who, purely by chance, opens a copy of an accursed tome. Jennings has, apparently, no sinful motive for his researches; he has simply blundered into a forbidden zone, the degrading fascination presumably a result, not a cause, of his studies. He finds himself imperiled, like Frankenstein, but with no willful intention by "things man was not meant to know."* Sullivan may be correct in saying that "the derangement of Jennings's mind is a mirror image of a derangement in the cosmos" (Sullivan, 21). In this kind of universe the victim need not do anything to invite his doom; simply *knowing* is enough to seal his fate.

The haunting in "The Familiar" has a more traditional ghost-story motive. Captain Barton is apparently dogged and finally destroyed by the ghost of a sailor formerly under his command; Barton had debauched the sailor's daughter and then caused the man's death by harsh treatment. This background information, however, is not revealed until the last two pages of the story. Barton appears as an upright citizen with a good service record, though "generally reserved, and occasionally even moody" ("The Familiar," 209). Although this case is also derived from Hesselius' records, the doctor is not the narrator. The editor, Hesselius' secretary, identifies the narrator as a clergyman named Thomas Herbert. In his prologue the editor quotes Hesselius' comments on the case, in which the doctor praises Herbert as a "venerable Irish Clergyman" who is an entirely "unexceptionable narrator" in the moral sphere; on medical points, however, the narrative is inadequate for purposes of diagnosis. The editor also criticizes the narrator, in this case for the "occasional stiffness and redundancy of his sentences" ("The Familiar," 208, 243). But unlike his treatment of the manuscript source of "Green Tea," in "The Familiar" the editor affirms that he "has not altered one letter of the original text" ("The Familiar," 243). Since we have no grounds for doubting this claim, we can assume that the main body of the tale contains all that the narrator knows of the case. Much of his knowledge, though, is second-hand; though he has been "intimately acquainted with some of the actors in this strange drama," he admits that in writing the story he combines information from "various sources" ("The Familiar," 209). The principal sources seem to be General Montague (Barton's prospective father-in-law) and a clergyman whom Barton consults. It is noteworthy that Montague transmits two pieces of testimony that he has received from other witnesses—a maid who sees the

---

*Forbidden knowledge is a commonplace of Gothic fiction, from Emily's black veil through *Frankenstein, Melmoth,* and beyond. In the nineteenth century this kind of knowledge may be an analogue to the new scientific discoveries threatening to overturn what is left of the traditional world view; as someone is supposed to have said of evolution—"if it is true, we must make sure no one finds out."

ghost and a manservant who finds Barton's body. These particular incidents are, therefore, already hearsay when they reach Herbert, as are most of Barton's own comments on his condition. The Rev. Herbert does enter the story briefly, in chapter 3, as a character and sees the supposed ghost with his own eyes. All he can testify to is that an odd-looking man is following Barton; the nature of the harassment remains conjectural.

The editor places this tale in the same category as "Green Tea," despite the obvious difference between being haunted by a ghost for revenge and being haunted by a demon for no clear reason. Dr. Hesselius' note explains Barton's case in much the same way as Jennings' case. He classifies such cases in three groups, which roughly correspond to the three ways of explaining supernatural events listed at the beginning of chapter 4:

> Of those whose senses are alleged to be subject to supernatural impressions—some are simply visionaries, and propagate the illusions of which they complain, from diseased brain or nerves. Others are, unquestionably, infested by, as we term them, spiritual agencies, exterior to themselves. Others, again, owe their sufferings to a mixed condition. The interior sense, it is true, is opened; but it has been and continues open by the action of disease. ("The Familiar," 208)

Again Hesselius' insistence on the term "disease" impresses the reader as reductive. He displays overweening self-confidence in his assurance that if he had been able to question Barton, "I should have without difficulty referred those phenomena to their proper disease" ("The Familiar," 209). Barton himself is much less willing than Jennings to ascribe his experiences to supernatural agency. When Barton first hears footsteps behind him, he thinks they are an illusion. When he receives a threatening note from an anonymous "Watcher" (chapter 2), he suspects a hoax, not a ghost. After Barton succumbs to superstitious terror, other characters attempt to supply natural explanations for his experiences. The narrator describes an appearance of the ghost while Barton is under the influence of alcohol, though Herbert is quick to deny that the Captain has ingested enough wine to affect his mind. General Montague confronts Barton's trouble with a hearty, commonsense, laughably inadequate response. He is convinced that the ghost is a merely human nuisance who can be dealt with by physical force and the whole matter "cleared up, with a little attention and management, within a week at furthest." A darker irony is that Dr. Macklin, the clergyman to whom Barton appeals, also insists that his suffering must spring from "purely physical causes" ("The Familiar," 229, 224).

Barton is a freethinker, and there is some implication that his haunting is a punishment for his infidelity, as well as his misconduct toward the dead sailor. On the very evening of his first visitation he is shown heaping ridicule upon "the evidences of revelation" as well as "the supernatural and the marvellous." His ghastly experiences cause him to reconsider the supernatural in "a more candid and teachable spirit" ("The Familiar," 211, 224). When desperation drives him to the clergyman Dr. Macklin, although he urges Barton to pray to God, he does not admit the possibility of any lesser supernatural entities in the case. As for Barton, he is by this time fully convinced that "there is a God—a dreadful God—and that retribution follows guilt, in ways the most mysterious and stupendous," but he sees the "spiritual system" of the universe as "malignant" ("The Familiar," 224). Only when near death does he receive heavenly consolation, in a vision of the girl he ruined. Through her forgiveness (as Barton supposes) the ghostly persecution becomes an instrument of conversion.

Is the ghost in this story "real"? The weight of evidence in the narrative seems to favor the supernatural hypothesis over that of guilt-induced delusion. Several people see the apparition, real bullets are fired at Barton, and he receives threatening letters on tangible paper. (Could persecution by a live human being, as suggested by the commonsensical Montague, be the source of the "haunting"? At one point Barton even tries to convince himself that the supposedly dead sailor has somehow survived, but a physician pronounces that notion untenable.) On the other hand, Barton hears the ghost's voice in Macklin's presence, while Macklin hears nothing but the wind. The narrator maintains an attitude of agnosticism toward the ghost. His final paragraph reads:

> Whether these circumstances in reality bear, or not, upon the occurences of Barton's after-life, it is, of course, impossible to say. It seems, however, more than probable that they were at least, in his own mind, closely associated with them. But however the truth may be, as to the origin and motives of this mysterious persecution, there can be no doubt that, with respect to the agencies by which it was accomplished, absolute and impenetrable mystery is like to prevail until the day of doom. ("The Familiar," 243)

Nothing could be more unlike Dr. Hesselius' simplistic assurance. The very syntax, with its proliferation of parenthetical phrases and clauses, conveys hesitation. In the very midst of stating that "there can be no doubt," the narrator conveys nothing but doubt.

One purpose of this hesitation in Victorian ghost stories may be to enable the reader to enjoy the *frisson* of the supernatural while leaving an escape clause for his discursive intellect. In Le Fanu's fiction the medical secretary compiles his tales for an implied reader who maintains a contemplative distance from the subject matter, not one who expects his world view to be shaken by the act of reading. Hesselius' secretary chooses his stories (out of the doctor's vast collection of cases) for their ability "to amuse or horrify a lay reader" ("Green Tea," 179). Entertainment, not instruction, is offered; in fact, we are led to expect emotional titillation. The methodical arrangement of testimony, with the source of each item identified, implies that the reader is not disposed to believe in the supernatural and must be convinced—and still requires an alternative scientific explanation to aid his suspension of disbelief. "Carmilla" offers no escape clause at the conclusion, but resolves itself into a tale of the marvelous. Earlier parts of the story, however, employ mediated narration and other devices of fantastic discourse. Again the tale is introduced by Hesselius' editor. In this case he has not altered the manuscript entrusted to Hesselius by the narrator, Laura. He praises her as an "intelligent lady," "clever and careful," who writes with "conscientious particularity" ("Carmilla," 274). He has never met or corresponded with her, however, since she died before he discovered her manuscript among the doctor's papers. The overall tone of the manuscript, especially the references in the final paragraph to the length of time required for Laura to recover from her frightful experience, emphasizes the considerable lapse (eight years) between the events and her recording of them. Within Laura's narrative, documents and interpolated stories assume importance. All eyewitness evidence of Carmilla's vampiric nature rests, for Laura, on the testimony of others. For instance, General Spielsdorf, a friend of the family, narrates the death of his foster-daughter Bertha at the hands of a vampire who answers to Carmilla's description and appeared at the General's home in the same kind of mysterious way Carmilla was introduced to Laura's family (chapters 11–14). The General's charge against Carmilla is corroborated by the eccentric vampire hunter Baron Vordenburg, who is guided by the journals of a remote ancestor who had been involved with the vampire Countess. Laura does not witness the gory execution of the vampire in her coffin, but summarizes it from "the report of the Imperial Commission, with the signatures of all who were present at these proceedings, attached in verification of the statement" ("Carmilla," 336). On such an extraordinary subject, official certification is needed to compel belief. Laura is convinced of her friend's vampirism and pronounces with considerable emphasis:

> If human testimony, taken with every care and solemnity, judicially, before commissions innumerable, each consisting of many members, all chosen for integrity and intelligence, and constituting reports more voluminous perhaps than exist upon any one other class of cases, is worth anything, it is difficult to deny, or even to doubt the existence of such a phenomenon as the vampire. ("Carmilla," 335)

The catalogue of obsessively multiplied safeguards draws attention to the "if" and the "doubt."

Laura's firsthand evidence of Carmilla's nature is confined to the fact that after Carmilla disappeared from the household, Laura's "nightly sufferings" ceased ("Carmilla," 335). The rest of Laura's experiences are dubious. She suffers from strange dreams. She recalls a childhood encounter with a mysterious lady that may or may not have been a dream. Upon their first meeting, Carmilla tells Laura that she, in childhood, dreamed of Laura. (Since the dreams are mirror images of each other, Carmilla is in a sense Laura's double.) The striking correspondence of the dreams or visions is not conclusive evidence of a supernatural tie, for Laura might be back-projecting Carmilla's face into an obscure memory. After Carmilla's arrival Laura begins to dream of a fierce black animal and of Carmilla drenched in blood; she also feels, as she becomes ill, strange sensations in sleep. All these phenomena could be purely subjective. Laura suspects no evil of her friend at the time. In fact, she wakes from one nightmare "possessed with the one idea that Carmilla was being murdered" ("Carmilla," 308). The narrative plants several bits of misdirection that suggest Carmilla herself is victim rather than predator. She is languid and melancholy, and like Laura she purchases a charm to guard against the disease (i.e., vampirism) ravaging the neighborhood.

Carmilla's expressed opinions contribute to the misdirection. Though baptized, she hates religious ceremonies (as one would expect of a vampire) and speaks like a freethinker, except for her belief about death. She extols lovers who "die together, so that they may live together." Yet she scoffs at superstition, attributing the virtue of the charm she wears to nature, not magic. To Laura's father's invocation of God's care, she retorts, "Creator! *Nature!* . . . All things proceed from Nature—don't they?" ("Carmilla," 297). On the other hand, she professes to be frightened by ghost stories.

The contradictions in her attitudes extend to her behavior, sometimes languid, sometimes fiercely passionate. Laura is alternately attracted and repelled by her. Carmilla's passion "was like the ardour of a lover; it embarrassed me; it was hateful and yet overpowering" ("Carmilla," 292). At other times Laura is fond of Carmilla, yet cannot help suspecting her of some sort of intermittent insanity. The homosexual implications are obvious and, like the sexual element in *Dracula,* have little direct bearing on our study. Carmilla's perverse sexuality—as Laura sees it—may, however, reflect upon her invocation of "Nature" and the definition of the unnatural. In contrast to the traditional belief that human beings are divinely created with a certain determinate nature, of which some acts are violations, characters like Melmoth, Carmilla, Lytton's Margrave, and Dracula seem to hold the Sadean position that whatever is, is part of nature, including homosexuality and the blasphemous quest for physical immortality. The relevant point is that the hesitation in this story is not so much cognitive (though that element is present) as emotional—between loving and fearing Carmilla. Even after the sensational conclusion, this suspension between two contradictory passions remains. Writing at a distance of years, Laura says that "to this hour the image of Carmilla returns to memory with ambiguous alternations—sometimes the playful, languid, beautiful girl; sometimes the writhing fiend I saw in the ruined church." The phrase "writhing fiend," by the way, does not accurately describe what Laura has seen in the ruined chapel, a fleeting glimpse of "an instantaneous and horrible transformation" in Carmilla's features ("Carmilla," 339, 332). The small discrepancy casts a retrospective shadow on

Laura's ability to report her ordeal objectively even at a distance. Perhaps she recounts the experience in order to validate it for herself. The young Laura, like Frankenstein, is "studiously kept in ignorance of ghost stories, of fairy tales, and of all such lore as makes us cover up our heads when the door creaks suddenly." With such preparation she must react to her own supernatural experience as she expects Dr. Hesselius to react: "I am now going to tell you something so strange that it will require all your faith in my veracity to believe my story" ("Carmilla," 277, 278). The methodical particularity in the opening pages of her tale lays the groundwork for faith in her veracity, but the accumulation of detail may serve to convince herself as well as Hesselius, for the phenomenon of vampirism contradicts what she has been taught of the nature of reality. And her choice of the occult doctor as narratee may indicate a need to have her memories credited and confirmed by a figure of authority.

Allen Fenwick, protagonist of Lytton's *A Strange Story,* seems to act as his own narratee. He tells himself the story of his own progress through skepticism and ambiguity to faith. Or perhaps he addresses the narrative to others who hold the same mistaken world view embraced by his younger self. The nature of evidence, the distinction between fact and imagination, and the boundaries between the natural and supernatural are here, as in "Carmilla," of first importance. Allen's educative ordeal is effected by a typical Gothic villain, Margrave, a melodramatic, enigmatic figure who has, indeed, quite a bit in common with Melmoth. Both are wanderers; both have attained unnatural length of life by occult means; both are fascinated by innocence and bent on corrupting it. Margrave begins life (presumably) as Louis Grayle, an occultist hungry for power and immortality. In Aleppo he murders Haroun, a wise, good mystic, for the secret of the Elixir of Life. Under the name of Margrave, the murderer takes up residence in the village where the narrator, young Allen Fenwick, practices as a physician. Sir Philip Derval, Margrave's nemesis, happens to live in the same community, and Margrave kills Derval by preternatural means, then implicates Fenwick in the crime. Margrave is intensely interested in Allen's fiancée Lilian, hoping to use her as a clairvoyant. After Margrave lures Lilian away by night, in a somnambulistic trance, Fenwick marries her and takes her to Australia, to protect her health and reputation. There they encounter Margrave again. The magician coerces Fenwick to help him with the brewing of a new supply of the Elixir, but the process goes wrong, causing Margrave's death.

Lytton explicitly states this novel's didactic purpose, to awaken the reader to realities beyond the material. His preface covers the subject at some length. He defends the use of supernatural machinery in fiction, citing examples from ancient epic, Shakespeare, and other venerable sources. No sense of discontinuity accompanies his implicit comparison of Margrave to Homeric deities and Hamlet's father. Lytton claims an exalted ancestry for his tale of occult terror to prepare us for the spiritual transformation these outré experiences produce in his protagonist. He holds that "a supernatural agency is indispensable to the conception of the Epic," because "the Epic is the highest and the completest form in which Art can express either Man or Nature," and "without some gleams of the supernatural, Man is not man, nor Nature, nature" (*A Strange Story,* 1: ix). This paradox makes it clear that Lytton is writing from within a world view that conceives nature as derivative, not self-existent. Hence he is free to exalt romance over realism. Since "Philosophy and Romance both take their origin in the Principle of Wonder," in this story "Romance, through the freest exercise of its wildest vagaries, conducts its bewildered hero towards the same goal to which Philosophy leads its luminous Student" (*A Strange Story,* 1: vi). The author thus alerts the reader to receive Allen Fenwick's narrative as a spiritual autobiography, a journey from error to truth. Like Robinson Crusoe, Allen presents the errors of his early life, the doom inevitably consequent upon his spiritual blindness, and the conversion growing out of his ordeal. (Allen, though, never achieves Crusoe's degree of certainty.) Lytton maintains that supernatural machinery is suitable for "all works of imagination, in which Art looks on Nature with Man's inner sense of a something beyond and above her" (*A Strange Story,* 1: x). Here Lytton is referring not just to philosophy, but to religion—indeed, he tells us, to Christianity, which takes into account the whole man, not only the physical being. Edwin M. Eigner calls fiction like Lytton's, designed "to express . . . a visionary understanding of life," metaphysical romance (Eigner, *The Metaphysical Novel in England and America,* 171). Novelists of this school were openly didactic, bent on disproving the realists' world view and awakening the reader to the validity of idealism. The typical metaphysical romance presents experience "in purely materialistic or associational or positivistic terms, which are then contradicted from the idealist point of view so that experience is mystically transformed and a new reality is established" (Eigner, 9). In *A Strange Story* reality is initially shown in materialistic terms not only in a philosophic sense, but also in a moral sense; Allen Fenwick's main concerns are succeeding in his profession and establishing himself as a solid resident of the very ordinary village he serves (a setting more appropriate for social satire than supernatural terror). We shall see how Allen, through his encounter with Margrave's powers, comes to accept the world of the spirit and is converted from materialism to Christianity.

Lytton's attack on materialism is indirectly related to the crisis in belief engendered by nineteenth-century science, as illustrated by the characterization of Allen as a scientific investigator. In some sense, as we have seen, a crisis in belief was endemic from the seventeenth century on. But the new philosophy of the seventeenth and eighteenth centuries did not threaten the religious world view in the same sense as did the mechanistic science of the nineteenth. The Enlightenment's quest for universally valid truths included a search for a universal religion attainable by the unaided light of reason. As Radcliffe (for example) illustrates, in the earlier period reason and faith were assumed to be allies. Such was not the case in Lytton's time. As a nineteenth-century scientist, Allen begins with an erroneously mechanistic idea of the physical universe and particularly of human nature. Joseph I. Fradin associates *A Strange Story* with the challenge of Darwinism. The amoral Margrave, he suggests, epitomizes the monster that purely animal man would be. Man, in fact, cannot be purely animal; Margrave instead becomes demonic. In reaction to Darwinism, Lytton dramatized the problem of whether man evolved from lower life forms could "have an eternal spark in him" and "where among the blind processes of Nature was there room for God?" (Fradin, "The Absorbing Tyranny of Every-day Life," 5). Allen, as ethical man, stands one step higher than Margrave, amoral man, for Allen, at least, tries to live by the "light of intellect" (Fradin, 8). But Allen uses his intellect for dangerous purposes, attempting to disprove God and the soul. The gradual conquest of Allen's blindness unfolds in a milieu that juxtaposes a "magic wand with tea and crumpets" (Fradin, 5)—the occult with the commonplace reality admitted by mechanistic materialism. Fradin considers Lytton's attempt to translate the occult into scientific terms a failure of nerve, an instance of hedging. In my view Lytton deliberately combines science and the supernatural in order to show that belief in the realm of the spirit remains valid in an era of rapidly advancing physical science, that, in fact, the spiritual world view covers the facts of experience more thoroughly than a purely physical one. Instead of attaining this faith through some divine epiphany, Lytton's hero is converted by exposure to the "lower" supernatural.

The importance this novel assigns to the question of belief in the supernatural is made clear by the elaborate characterization of Allen as a skeptic. This characterization is the focus of the novel's early chapters, which, as in most metaphysical romances, portray "the alienation of which the skeptical world-view was both cause and symptom" (Eigner, 213). Lytton's protagonist is almost belligerently skeptical, his obdurate resistance lending more conviction to the mystical transformation; if this extreme materialist is converted, the evidence must be strong. Allen is so zealous against superstition that he publishes a pamphlet attacking an older colleague, Dr. Lloyd, for his belief in phenomena such as "somnambular clairvoyance" (*A Strange Story,* 1: 26). Driven to an early grave by the controversy, Lloyd bestows a deathbed curse on Allen. The young doctor, though he still thinks himself justified in satirizing ridiculous notions, pays public respect to Lloyd's memory and even takes up a subscription for his orphaned children. Allen appears quite smug about this philanthropic act. He accuses himself of intellectual pride, a charge borne out by the attitudes he describes himself as holding. After cataloguing his mental and physical assets at length, he summarizes, "Thus the sense of a robust individuality, strong alike in disciplined reason and animal vigor—habituated to aid others, needing no aid for itself—contributed to render me impervious in will and arrogant in opinion" (*A Strange Story,* 1: 25). The narrative is retrospective, not "written to the moment"; Allen foreshadows the changes that will overtake him in remarks like, "Such at the time I now speak of were the views I held" (*A Strange Story,* 1: 24). He inundates the reader with details of his personal and professional prosperity and his insufferable self-confidence, rendering all too obvious the hubris of which his younger self is guilty. His imminent downfall is glaringly inevitable.

Falling in love strikes the first blow against his rational materialism. Though a firm disbeliever in romantic love, Allen is enamoured at first sight of Lilian, a delicate girl of clairvoyant tendencies, accustomed all her life to seeing visions. She represents the idealized character-type Eigner calls the "domestic angel," whose purity helps to lead the protagonist out of the bondage of his errors (Eigner, 120). Lilian's account of her late father's spirit commending her to Allen's care before they have ever met does not seriously disturb his skepticism. He has his first supernatural experience shortly after this conversation, ironically while working on a monograph opposing the theory of innate ideas. (Lytton's ironies are hardly subtle.) Allen is visited by a pale, silvery, vaguely human shape. Only momentarily taken aback, he dismisses the apparition as suitable for inclusion in his "Chapter on the Cheats of the Senses and Spectral Phantasms" (*A Strange Story,* 1: 142). In contrast to the protagonists of eighteenth-century Gothic romances, prone to mistake illusions and hoaxes for specters, Allen persists in classifying genuine supernatural experiences as illusory. When he attends Sir Philip Derval's steward, who claims to have seen the wraith of his absent master, Allen gives no credence to the apparition. Allen later meets Derval, who places him in a trance and shows him a vision of Margrave, outwardly young but actually ancient and indwelt by a vital spark of animal intelligence devoid of soul. This experience is the first crack in Allen's armor; he cries, "Have I ever then doubted that soul is distinct from mind?" But as soon as he recovers, he proceeds to rationalize his vision, ashamed of being "so helpless a puppet" and "so morbidly impressed by phantasmagorical illusions." Even when the shadow-specter of Margrave speaks to Allen, the latter addresses it as, "Fiend or spectre, or mere delusion of my own brain" (*A Strange Story,* 1: 256, 257, 347). Later he goes so far as to use a magic wand he has found, but all the while reproaching himself for superstitious weakness. His devotion to scientific rationalism, paradoxically, leads him to ignore the testimony of his senses. When he finds himself "in this practical nineteenth century ... prying into long-neglected corners and dust-holes of memory for what my reason had rejected as worthless rubbish," he cannot bring himself to consider this "prying" as other than "folly" (*A Strange Story,* 1: 387). (Notice Allen's explicit—and defensive—emphasis on "this practical nineteenth century.") Lytton's novel is one instance of a category of fantastic fiction in which the reader tends to accept the supernatural phenomena before the protagonist does. Allen's preternatural ordeal, combined with estrangement from Lilian and an arrest for Derval's murder (reminiscent of the persecutions inflicted on Stanton and Moncada), begins to erode his skepticism. His immediate reaction is a kind of nihilistic despair:

> It would be ludicrously absurd to suppose that Dr. Lloyd's dying imprecation could have had a prophetic effect upon my destiny—to believe that the pretences of mesmerisers were specially favored by Providence, and that to question their assumptions was an offence of profanation to be punished by exposure to preternatural agencies. There was not even that congruity between cause and effect which fable seeks in excuse for its inventions. (*A Strange Story*, 1: 367)

Allen criticizes his own life as inartistic. His sufferings, like Jennings' in "Green Tea," are underdetermined. Like Moncada and Don Carlos, Allen finds his life manipulated by a force that mirrors the function of the author—but an inept author, one who trivializes his characters' experience by neglecting to supply the requisite "congruity between cause and effect." Though his life (to his outrage) comes to resemble a romance, it fails to conform to romance's generic conventions.

Two characters, the adventurer and occultist Sir Philip Derval and Allen's mentor, Dr. Julius Faber, fill the occult doctor role in this novel. Derval, a disciple of the slain mystic of Aleppo, believes in clairvoyance, preternatural trances, and the Elixir of Life. He preaches the reality of "three states of existence—the animal, the mental, the spiritual," which he compares to the states of matter (*A Strange Story*, 1: 240). This kind of theory is aptly characterized by Eigner as "modern occultism, washed clean of its diabolical associations" (Eigner, 190). Allen considers these beliefs, not to mention the credence Derval gives to Grayle/Margrave's power to control other men and even demons, as purely superstitious. Faber's attitude toward strange phenomena is more orthodox, though less dogmatic than Allen's. Faber will never "peremptorily deny what I have not witnessed" (*A Strange Story*, 2: 174), in contrast to Allen, who obstinately denies what he *has* witnessed. Faber's response to Allen's apparently supernatural experiences, however, is somewhat less than adequate; he attributes them to association of ideas, overwork, and dreams. Seemingly independent testimony to the apparition of Margrave's shadow-self he assigns to "a common family likeness" among all such "hallucinations." He insists that it is "more philosophical" to "leave the extraordinary unaccounted for" than to admit "an explanation which accepts the supernatural" (*A Strange Story*, 2: 23, 24). This agnosticism does not extend to revealed religion. Unlike Allen, Faber believes in God and the soul, and he rebukes Allen for his narrow-mindedness in that area. He tells Allen to burn his monograph, read the Bible, and pray. Allen has so thoroughly accepted Faber's arguments about the supernatural that he rejects this advice on the ground that following it would make him more vulnerable to superstition.

The problematic nature of Allen's experiences is foregrounded by various narrative devices. (As Eigner points out, a mixture of narrative techniques is characteristic of metaphysical romance, for a nonlinear, retarding structure keeps the reader distanced from the protagonist's predicament and alert to the author's arguments.) Within Allen's retrospective story are embedded second-hand reports from other sources. Oral accounts of Grayle/Margrave's past come from Mrs. Poyntz, a local matriarch, and a Prussian count whom Allen meets in Australia. Oral testimony to the wizard's role in Derval's murder is transmitted by Allen's housekeeper and by the escaped lunatic who actually strikes the fatal blow (though neither account is fully credited by the skeptical Allen, of course). A written memoir left by Derval holds a central position in the story. Allen is assigned the task of editing this posthumous narrative and enjoined to suppress any parts judged too dangerous for humanity to know. Like John Melmoth before him and, after him, Hesselius' secretary and several characters in *Dracula,* Allen as editor must sift through documentary evidence to uncover truths that will shape his own view of reality. He is interrupted, in the midst of reading the manuscript, by Margrave's shadow, and afterward the paper has vanished. The disappearance of this document involves Allen in legal difficulties and, more important for the novel's theme, makes it impossible for him to consult the memoir later to reconfirm what he has read. The content of the manuscript (to the point he was interrupted) rests only on his memory, and he no longer trusts his own perceptions.

The reliability of testimony, whether oral or written, is questioned within the text. A footnote to Derval's memoir points out that his account of the duel in which Grayle was involved differs from Mrs. Poyntz's. The editor (as Lytton styles himself when appearing *in propria persona* outside the preface) says, "Sir Philip's account must, at least, be nearer the truth than the lady's," and cites legal statutes to support that contention. The editor also praises Allen for leaving the reader to draw his own conclusions from this contradiction. Here Lytton compares the "rapidity with which truth becomes transformed into fable" to the familiar parlor game in which a sentence is whispered from one player to the next, becoming distorted in the process (*A Strange Story,* 313). Doubt is being cast on the narrative's reliability by the most authoritative source within it. Allen, on the other hand, attempts to convince the reader of his dependability as a witness; he describes his memory as "habitually tenacious even in ordinary matters, and strained to the utmost extent of its power, by the strangeness of the ideas presented to it" (*A Strange Story,* 1: 323). Yet in the end he confesses his inability to explain or understand his preternatural experiences. After the wild ritual that ends in Margrave's death, Allen, now a believer in God, says:

> How trivial now became the weird riddles that, a little while before, had been clothed in so solemn an awe!... Doubtless the sights and sounds which had haunted the last gloomy

night, the calm reason of Faber would strip of their magical seemings;—the Eyes in the space and the Foot in the circle might be those of no terrible Demons, but of the wild's savage children. (*A Strange Story*, 2: 342–43)

Fearing that Lilian may be lost to him forever, Allen reflects, "Man alone, of all earthly creatures, asks, 'Can the Dead die forever?' and the instinct that urges the question is God's answer to man!" Though science may eventually find explanations for all apparently supernatural portents, the true mystery of the universe is "the wonders of God," which will remain forever beyond man's wisdom (*A Strange Story*, 2: 341, 343). Hence Allen manages to retain his scientific outlook while accepting the spiritual realm with humbled faith. Eigner rejects the hypothesis that the metaphysical novelists intend to leave the reader with an impression of "open-ended ambiguity" (Eigner, 175). Why, then, does the protagonist of *A Strange Story* not arrive at a conclusion about the precise nature of Margrave's "sorcery" and the attendant apparitions? Eigner maintains that "we cannot be instructed beyond confusion as to which vision of reality the author really wants us to accept," because such a program "would interpret the metaphysical dream or visionary moment, thereby reducing it again to mere allegory." He concludes that these novelists "contented themselves by presenting their preferred and uninterpreted world-view last in the sequence" (*A Strange Story*, 227). On this hypothesis Allen's final meditation ought to express Lytton's own philosophy.

A Strange Story concerns, in Derval's words, the "border-land between natural science and imaginative speculation" (*A Strange Story*, 2: 307). So, in its own way, does Bram Stoker's *Dracula*. (This novel resembles Lytton's in curious ways that have no direct bearing on our subject—the similarities between Margrave and Dracula, between Derval and Van Helsing, between Margrave's seduction of Lilian and Dracula's of Lucy, between Margrave's manipulation of the homicidal lunatic and Dracula's of Renfield.) More than any other fiction we have considered, *Dracula* epitomizes the relation between the fantastic and narrative structure. It makes the documents themselves, with the question of the reliability of oral and written testimony, a central theme. Stoker handles the documentary structure expertly, rarely falling into the Richardsonian trap of unrealistically long letters or journal entries. Yet he shares with Richardson an immediacy arising from the moment-to-moment recounting of events by narrators to whom the outcome is still unknown. Stoker's realism of presentation and his familiar setting make the tale more immediately vivid to the reader than most Gothic romances. Like the eighteenth-century Gothics that introduce essentially modern characters into a medieval setting, Stoker portrays the infringement of an alien terror from the past upon a tidy contemporary world. He also foregrounds the problem of the reality of the supernatural as it impinges upon faith and sanity. In many ways *Dracula* is the culmination of the fantastic-Gothic mode.

Bram Stoker, an 1885 Sketch

Stoker's Vampire of the Mind

Most of the studies of Bram Stoker's *Dracula* (1897) so far published concentrate upon its subliminal sexual content. Two scholars, however, Carol A. Senf and David Seed, have extensively treated Stoker's narrative technique. Senf asserts that this technique foregrounds "the subjective nature of the story which his narrators relate" (Senf, *"Dracula,"* 161). The point of her article, however, is the novel's supposed blurring of the boundaries between good and evil (a view with which I partly agree), and she, like most readers, concludes that *Dracula*'s main theme is repressed sexuality and violence. Seed analyzes *Dracula* in narrative order, demonstrating how the form of each section facilitates Stoker's purpose of first plunging characters and reader into mysteries that defy rational explanation, then fragmenting the characters' perceptions and distancing them from "the true nature of events" (Seed, "The Narrative Method of *Dracula*," 74), and finally filling the gaps in their perception to make possible the vampire's overthrow. One other critic, Mark M. Hennelly, like Senf, connects the novel's moral conflict with its narrative structure. This intriguing article departs from the usual psychosexual preoccupation to suggest that *Dracula* is "an allegory of rival epistemologies in quest of a gnosis which will rehabilitate the Victorian wasteland" (Hennelly, *"Dracula,"* 13). Yet this author, building his reading upon what he sees as a conflict of epistemologies *within* the novel, does not deal with epistemology as a structural principle *of* the novel. Stoker's complex epistolary structure, employing a variety of subjective reports, suggests that the nature of truth, reality, and belief is itself the novel's central theme.*

---

*Senf and Hennelly are not the only critics to find ambiguity in *Dracula*. Two articles on the psychosexual theme, "Feminism, Sex Role Exchanges, and Other Subliminal Fantasies in Bram Stoker's *Dracula*," by Stephanie Demetrakopoulos, and "Suddenly Sexual Women in Bram Stoker's *Dracula*," by Phyllis A. Roth, call into question the goodness of the "good" characters (so insisted upon by Stoker's surface remarks), as does Senf. Another article, *"Dracula:* Bram Stoker's Spoiled Masterpiece," by Royce MacGillivray, draws attention to the complexity of the novel's narrative structure as its strongest point. Leonard Wolf's introduction to *The Annotated Dracula* says that the book "gives wildly contradictory signals about what kind of a work it is" (Wolf, ix). My own earlier study of vampirism in literature, *Shadow of a Shade* (New York: Gordon Press, 1975), touches only briefly on the issues raised in this chapter, instead concentrating on Stoker's place in the historical development of vampire fiction.

Among the questions confronting the characters are: (a) Is the experience of vampirism a genuine supernatural phenomenon or a delusion? (b) Granted its reality, is vampirism simply a tool of Satan or a destructive, inhuman but morally neutral force? Jonathan Harker, Dracula's guest, when recovered from his nervous breakdown, explains to Professor Van Helsing:

> I was in doubt, and then everything took a hue of unreality, and I did not know what to trust, even the evidence of my own senses. Not knowing what to trust, I did not know what to do; and so had only to keep on working in what had hitherto been the groove of my life. The groove ceased to avail me, and I mistrusted myself. Doctor, you don't know what it is to doubt everything, even yourself. (*Dracula,* 170)

Doubt—of oneself, one's sanity, and the objective universe—is the dominant motif of *Dracula.*

One may take the contrary view that the numerous documents contributing to the story of the vampire Count, presented from various points of view in multiple voices, render the heroes' position credible and aim at certainty rather than doubt. Why does *Dracula* not produce the same comforting vision of the universe that we find in Radcliffe's romances? Radcliffe's artificial terrors ultimately convey the impression that the universe is a safe place, because God protects the virtuous from any serious harm. *Dracula,* on the other hand, bristles with hints that God is not quite in control. Van Helsing tells his allies, "Thus are we ministers of God's own wish: that the world, and men for whom His Son die, will not be given over to monsters, whose very existence would defame Him" (*Dracula,* 282). The conditional "would" sounds peculiar, since, according to Van Helsing, vampires *do* exist. As Leonard Wolf says, "What does this do to God's fame?" (*Dracula,* 282). Other passages likewise imply that God's power over evil has limitations. Lucy, although overtly an innocent victim throughout her involvement with Dracula, becomes a demonic figure under his influence. Dr. Seward calls the vampire Lucy "the foul Thing which had taken Lucy's shape without her soul" and "a nightmare of Lucy" (*Dracula,* 192). Yet Stoker does not present vampirism as the possession of a corpse by an alien entity, as some authors do; the fiendish Lucy is Lucy herself transformed. If she can be involuntarily changed into a demon by Dracula, one may suspect that the vampire's power rivals God's (since He cannot defend those loyal to Him against the very loss of their souls). Mina, as well, though virtuous, becomes "unclean," bearing a "mark of shame," even though she has been "polluted" by Dracula against her own will (*Dracula,* 263). A world where such things can happen to the innocent is hardly as secure and consolatory as Radcliffe's world.

Science fiction writer Anthony Boucher characterizes Van Helsing, the *raisonneur* who claims to deliver the definitive truth about their world to the other characters in *Dracula,* as "a hard-headed scientist of the only century to believe that science knew everything" (Boucher, introduction to *Dracula*, ix). Stoker himself bombards us with reminders that his story's setting is "nineteenth century up-to-date with a vengeance" (*Dracula*, 38)—shorthand, typing, blood transfusions, telegrams, phonograph recordings, scientific criminology. These technological items, along with constant stress on mundane phenomena such as railway schedules (Dracula reads *Bradshaw's Guide*), maps, detailed guidebook-style observations of the dress and manners of Transylvania, the menu of Jonathan's first meal at Castle Dracula (along with his resolution to get the recipe for it—one instance of the recording compulsion common to all the characters), and even his shaving problems after Dracula smashes his only mirror, set the fantastic events in a highly realistic context. We are constantly reminded that the victims of these strange events (all the more jarringly alien and horrible in such a commonplace milieu) are our contemporaries and fellow citizens. We are invited to identify with the protagonists even as we recognize the alienating isolation that accompanies their slowly dawning belief in the incredible. When supernatural horror is juxtaposed with modern science and technology, with the "groove" of everyday life, skepticism and uncertainty are the expected responses. The evil represented by Dracula, to which the Christian and civilized good of the heroes is opposed, conforms to Fredric Jameson's formula for romance, in which "the concept of evil is at one with the category of Otherness itself: evil characterizes whatever is radically different from me" (Jameson, "Magical Narratives," 140). The very first paragraph of *Dracula* describes a movement from West to East, from a familiar to an alien world. In their first extended conversation the Count makes a point of reminding Jonathan, "Transylvania is not England," and of how Dracula himself in London will be "a stranger in a strange land" (*Dracula*, 24, 23). Here Jonathan (and later the other characters) confronts a reality that cannot be comprehended in the categories familiar to him. Such a confrontation is ideally suited to fantastic fiction.

The novel's introductory statement (by the editor, whether Stoker or Jonathan) stresses the story's radical "variance" from "the possibilities of later-day belief." This remark defines the anticipated reaction not only of potential readers within the story (Jonathan's contemporaries), but also of the implied reader whose role we assume. The fictional editor's narratee (presumably the sort of person who might come across this assemblage of documents in the course of research into the occult) may well be convinced, by the story's end, that vampires actually threaten contemporary England. This conviction will profoundly alter his world view and may have practical repercussions in his life (for instance, inducing him to seek out Van Helsing and volunteer for an anti-vampire crusade). The implied reader outside the text, on the other hand, is unlikely to find his nineteenth- (or twentieth-) century up-to-date skepticism shaken by the reading of a fiction that he recognizes throughout as fiction. (On this point Stoker may be contrasted with Lytton, who apparently does intend his fiction, though acknowledged as such, to effect a real-world change in the reader's attitude.) Because of his advantage of multiple perspective, he accepts Dracula's reality within the tale more readily than the characters do, while maintaining (if a typical representative of modern Western culture) an absolute disbelief in vampires outside the fiction. Entertaining, for the duration of the reading experience, a provisional and hypothetical belief in the Undead, he may contemplate the dissonance between the universe as he conceives it and as it would be if the story's events were in fact possible.

We recall Todorov's observation that in the fantastic the hesitation between "a natural and supernatural explanation of the events described," as it is represented through a character or characters, "becomes one of the themes of the work" (Todorov, *The Fantastic,* 33). It is this property of the fantastic that I particularly wish to apply to *Dracula.* In keeping with Jonathan's legal profession and preoccupations, evidence and proof are all-important in this story, but as long as the fantastic is sustained, no proof can be sufficient. The narrative is kept in the realm of the fantastic by several devices: (a) As Senf points out, the whole novel is framed by an introductory note and an epilogue that explicitly call attention to the incredibility of the tale narrated (Senf, 161). In the epilogue Jonathan actually says, "It was almost impossible to believe that the things which we had seen with our own eyes and heard with our own ears were living truths" (*Dracula,* 332). This kind of assertion is repeated too often to be the purely formal outburst of astonishment typical of most horror fiction. (b) The characters constantly question their own and each other's sanity; madness is, in fact, a far more obtrusive motif than sexuality. References to madness cease only with chapter 24, when the final pursuit of Dracula begins. (c) Many of the critical events are not presented directly to the reader, but are told by one character to another. (d) At least two of the written documents in the novel are treated as stories whose validity must be evaluated by the characters—Jonathan's diary (chapters 1–4) and the ship's log of the *Demeter* (chapter 7).

The last-mentioned item requires only brief attention. The experience recorded by the captain of the *Demeter* (a beautifully chosen name, with its resonance of return from the kingdom of Death) provides a good example of Stoker's use of indirect narrative. The relevant portions of the ship's log are first translated from Russian, then reproduced in a newspaper article, which, in turn, is presented to the reader as a clipping pasted into Mina's diary. Within the captain's story, furthermore, he is not so much reporting his own experience as recording the testimony of the deranged first mate. Only at the end of his account does the captain himself see face to face the shadowy being (presumably Dracula) terrorizing the ship. The finders of the derelict, deserted except for the captain's body, do not know how to respond to the mysterious tale. The newspaper article hesitates between two alternative readings: "There is no evidence to adduce; and whether the man himself committed the murders there is now none to say. The folk hold almost universally here that the captain is simply a hero" (*Dracula,* 87). For the characters with whom this section is concerned (mainly Mina and Lucy) there is at this time no way of determining whether the log records the captain's degeneration into homicidal mania or his heroic defense against a mysterious sequence of disasters. We as readers, being acquainted with Jonathan's diary, are in a better position to resolve the hesitation. As Seed says, the diary "gives readers a 'memory,' a store of images that enables them to interpret the fragmentary signs that fill characters' later accounts" (Seed, 65).

The problem of how to read Jonathan's journal takes on greater symbolic importance than the problem of the ship's log. First, as illustrated by his remark quoted above, Jonathan is tormented by doubts of the reality of his Transylvanian experience. With his memory of the horrible events obscured by the intervening "brain fever," his only possible access to the past lies in the journal he kept at Castle Dracula. But he chooses not to be told his own story: "I do not know if it was all real or the dreaming of a madman. . . . The secret is here, and I do not want to know it." The closed book symbolizes his self-doubt and the unreliability of memory. It also represents an element in the relationship between Jonathan and Mina, his bride. Holding firm ideas on "the trust between man and wife: there should be no secret, no concealment," Jonathan turns the notebook over to Mina, leaving her the choice of whether or not to read it. She, in turn, wraps, ties, and seals the book, as "an outward and visible sign" of their mutual trust (*Dracula,* 104). She promises never to read the journal "unless it were for his own dear sake or for the sake of some stern duty." When she does at last read the Transylvanian narrative, she has no means to evaluate its accuracy: "Did he get his brain fever and then write all those terrible things; or has he some cause for it all?" (*Dracula,* 105, 163). Mina as Jonathan's narratee (like the newspaper correspondent as reader of the *Demeter*'s log) might be expected to guide our response. Her reaction, though (like the reporter's reaction to the captain's testimony), does not have sufficient certainty to be authoritative for us as readers; unless we have already decided that Jonathan's breakdown *followed* his stay at Castle Dracula, we can only share her doubt. She deals with the threat of the journal's ambiguity in the same way that she later deals with the other documents in the case, by transcribing it on the typewriter. It is she who eventually reduces all the diverse bits of testimony to a single, uniform "mass of type-writing" (Day, *In the Circles of Fear and Desire,* 332). Once Jonathan's diary is standardized, as it were, in typescript, it becomes manageable, for it can be turned over to Van Helsing, who removes its threatening ambiguity by pronouncing it factual. All the characters, indeed, are obsessed with keeping accurate accounts (even the mad Renfield has his little notebook full of figures), to the point that Mina must transcribe and enter on record an intimate conversation between herself and Arthur, which has no direct relation to the vampire mystery (chapter 17). In chapter 21 Dracula tries to hamper the heroes' campaign by destroying their original records, and it is considered important that the typescript copy is intact and safely locked up. By subjecting their experiences of the supernatural to modern technology (typing and phonography), the characters seem to be trying to manage the horror, tame it, force it into the "groove" of ordinary life and out of the ambiguous realm of the fantastic. Concerning their collation of the heterogeneous documents, William Patrick Day says that "creation of the complete and coherent text is the analogue to the emergence of understanding that puts an end to Dracula" (Day, *In the Circles of Fear and Desire,* 57). The constant journal-keeping, moreover, seems to serve the two purposes of validating personal experience for the writer and providing concrete evidence for potential readers. Jonathan sets the keynote when he writes, early in the novel:

> Up to now I never quite knew what Shakespeare meant when he made Hamlet say:—
> "My tablets! quick, my tablets!
> 'Tis meet that I put it down," etc.
> for now, feeling as if my own brain were unhinged or as if the shock had come which must end in its undoing, I turn to my diary for repose. The habit of entering accurately must help to soothe me. (*Dracula,* 38)

Jonathan speaks as if his actual experience would evaporate into unreality if it were not written down. The words "repose" and "soothe" (as if the journal were a sort of tranquilizing drug) reflect his attempt to reduce cognitive dissonance and restore emotional homeostasis by containing the horror in a verbal pattern. Notice that the diary's soothing aspect is "the habit of entering accurately." The act of writing relegates the strange experience to a familiar pigeonhole (habit) and satisfies the rational intellect with ostensible accuracy.

As a lawyer, Jonathan is naturally preoccupied with assembling evidence to support his version of these extraordinary events. The quasi-legal format of the documentary case against Dracula recalls the connection (mentioned in chapter 1) between changing standards of legal proof in the seventeenth century and the technique of formal realism in the early novel. Jonathan's authorship of the novel's retrospective epilogue implies that he is the guiding hand behind the process of assembling the documents into a coherent narrative. And though the writer of the prefatory note is not identified, symmetry suggests (as does artistic consistency) that this voice is Jonathan's again, rather than Stoker's in an editorial persona. This editor, whether Jonathan or Stoker, makes clear his awareness of dealing with a skeptical audience. He calls the story "a history almost at variance with the possibilities of later-day belief" and concedes that all statements are "given from the standpoints and within the range of knowledge of those who made them." Multiple narrators thus become unavoidable, since gaps in one witness' knowledge must be filled by the testimony of another. Unlike witnesses in a courtroom, however, these narrators address themselves to a number of different narratees. Even Jonathan's journal, rather than being solely a private record for his own recollection, is intended partly for Mina (he makes a memo to write down a certain recipe for her, reflects on her probable reaction to his account of his lust for the female vampires, and apostrophizes her just before his desperate escape attempt), as her diary is for him. The various letters are adapted to their respective correspondents, and a newspaper report, working up facts into a sensational tale for the general public, differs sharply from both diaries and letters.

The hearsay evidence of Jonathan's journal and the ship's log is matched by several instances of verbal hearsay evidence, incidents told by one character to another secondhand. Dracula's true nature and activities are kept problematic partly because, after the first four chapters, we rarely see him face to face. Lucy does not directly narrate her experience of meeting Dracula for the first time, early in chapter 8, but a few pages later she describes the encounter to Mina as a cryptic dream of "something long and dark with red eyes...and something very sweet and very bitter all around me at once" (*Dracula*, 98). In chapter 11 a zookeeper describes, for a newspaper interview, Dracula's visit to the Zoological Gardens shortly before the escape of a wolf that becomes the vampire's tool in the final ruin of Lucy. In Lucy's memorandum of this climactic night, at the end of the chapter, Dracula does not even appear in person; his appearance is displaced into the newspaper article reporting the zookeeper's testimony. One of the novel's most intense scenes, Dracula's attack on Mina (chapter 21), is not reported by Mina, the central character, from whom we might expect the fullest and most accurate account. Instead, the tale appears in Dr. Seward's diary, told by Mina after the fact to the assembled men. Dracula's last appearance before leaving England is again a mediated one. Mina's diary reports Van Helsing's account of his interview with a Russian ship's captain who has seen the Count. Stoker seems deliberately to place as many filters as possible between the reader and the facts. Juliet Willman Kincaid remarks that Stoker "works hard to make his witnesses seem reliable," by using as narrators figures of authority such as scientists, lawyers, and newspaper reporters (Kincaid, "The Novel as Journal," 84). But of more interest is the way Stoker's mediated narrative *undermines* the traditional reliability of such sources.

Besides these important events relegated to secondhand narrative, the same treatment distinguishes two events that seem to have no essential plot function and, in fact, appear to retard the action. These occur in chapters 5 and 6, universally acknowledged as the dullest section of the novel, an abrupt letdown after the cliff-hanging (almost literally) conclusion of Jonathan's Transylvanian adventure. Montague Summers dismisses these two chapters as "the rather tedious courtships of Lucy Westenra" (Summers, *The Vampire*, 334). But analysis of the two interpolated stories I refer to, Lucy's account to Mina of her three proposals (chapter 5) and old Mr. Swales' tale of the suicide (chapter 6), reveals unobtrusive foreshadowings of many of the novel's dominant themes and images. The author is planting hints that may later be expected to resonate in the reader's unconscious.

In moving from Transylvania to England, we shift (for the time being) from the relatively unmediated reportage of Jonathan's diary to letters, whose content may be assumed to be more conditioned by awareness of an audience. We receive the facts of Lucy's courtships, not as raw data in Lucy's mind, but as a narrative she composes for her friend Mina, a fairy tale meant to end with "happily ever after." (The threefold proposal places Lucy in a folklore tradition whose darker side is embodied by the vampire motif.) Lucy's treatment of the three proposals does more than introduce three important characters (a task the author could have accomplished in less space); it also foreshadows the future destinies of Lucy and her suitors. We first notice the difference in the amount of space devoted to each of the men. Quincey Morris' proposal is treated at the greatest length, although he is arguably the most "minor" of the book's major characters. (He has been omitted from all but one of *Dracula's* film adaptations.) The full dialogue between Quincey and Lucy is recorded, while Dr. Seward's proposal is relegated to indirect discourse, and that of Arthur Holmwood (the favored suitor) is only summarized. This focus on Quincey is significant in view of the fact that he is the only one of the heroes to lose his life in the struggle against the vampire, and Jonathan and Mina's firstborn child is named after him. His farewell speech to Lucy, with its emphasis on darkness and the Last Judgment, hints at his coming death: "My dear, I'm going to have a pretty lonely walk between this and Kingdom Come. Won't you give me one kiss? It'll be something to keep off the darkness now and then" (*Dracula*, 62). Lucy's concluding remark about Dr. Seward, on the other hand, seems to foreshadow her own death. She tells Mina how sad it is to reject a man "whom you know loves you honestly... and to know that, no matter what he may say at the moment, you are passing quite out of his life" (*Dracula*, 60). This statement is ironic, since Lucy will soon pass out of Seward's life in a more terrible and final way than she can suspect.

Some of Lucy's other remarks look forward to her relationship with Dracula. At the beginning of her letter she gives Mina permission to repeat the tale of the three suitors to Jonathan, "because I would, if I were in your place, certainly tell Arthur. A woman ought to tell her husband everything"

(*Dracula,* 60). Yet when a few weeks later the vampire begins preying upon her, this secret remains concealed from her fiancé Arthur until after her "death." True, the concealment is not a willful act on Lucy's part, yet certain cryptic statements to Mina (especially page 95), as well as her seductive behavior on her deathbed, show that on some preconscious level she is aware of what is happening to her. In the next scene Lucy mentions the fascination of Quincey Morris' anecdotes of his adventurous past in America: "I sympathize with poor Desdemona, when she had such a dangerous stream poured in her ear" (*Dracula,* 61). In his note to this passage Leonard Wolf compares Dracula to Othello, whom Brabantio suspects of using some kind of sorcery to win Desdemona. We may go further than Wolf and state explicitly that Lucy at last spurns all her lawful suitors to form an unnatural union with a lover even more alien than a Moor. (Stoker's phrase "dangerous stream" may be intended to evoke an image of tainted blood.) Yet in a sense she does not reject any of these men. She laments to Mina, "Why can't they let a girl marry three men, or as many as want her, and save all this trouble?" (*Dracula,* 62). As Wolf also points out, by the multiple blood transfusions she undergoes Lucy symbolically weds all her suitors, as well as Dracula, so that (in Van Helsing's words) "this so sweet maid is a polyandrist" (*Dracula,* 159). Lucy, in short, tells herself and Mina the story of her life as she envisions it, but its fulfillment is thwarted in ironic and terrible ways.

The episode of Mr. Swales, the old Whitby seaman, serves no apparent function other than local color and is apt to be skipped in second and later readings of the novel. His gossip, however, behind the almost impenetrable Yorkshire dialect in which Stoker clothes it, prepares us for some of the novel's important events and themes. His conversation in chapter 6 consists mostly of ghastly-comic reflections on graveyards and the Judgment Day. He shows Lucy and Mina a number of empty graves (empty because their supposed occupants were lost at sea). "'Here lies the body' or 'Sacred to the memory' wrote on all of them, an' yet in nigh half of them there bean't no bodies at all" (*Dracula,* 68). Graves bearing names but no bodies hold a central place in this novel, notably Lucy's deserted crypt in chapter 16 and, near the end of the story, "one great tomb more lordly than all the rest. . . . On it was but one word: DRACULA" (*Dracula,* 324). Mr. Swales underscores his scorn for superstition and sentimentality alike by telling Lucy and Mina the truth about the grave over which their favorite seat in the churchyard is placed. The stone reads: "Sacred to the memory of George Canon, who died, in the hope of a glorious resurrection, on July 29, 1873, falling from the rocks at Kettleness. This tomb is erected by his sorrowing mother to her dearly beloved son. 'He was the only son of his mother, and she was a widow'" (*Dracula,* 70). (We may notice in passing that Lucy is also a widow's only child, the mode of whose death is not what it appears to be.) Swales tells the true story of George's life, revealing that the dead man was a cripple whose mother hated him and that he committed suicide to cheat her of his life insurance. Here the conflict of report with fact is foregrounded. If even the inscription on a grave, a matter of public record, preserved in the privileged setting of a churchyard, cannot be trusted, what can? What are we meant to think of all the other dubious reports in the novel? Suicide is reemphasized when Lucy protests: "Oh, why did you tell us of this? It is my favorite seat, and I cannot leave it; and now I find I must go on sitting over the grave of a suicide" (*Dracula,* 70). On this very spot, in fact, Lucy first yields to Dracula's kiss—a liason between the living and the dead foreshadowed by Mr. Swales' jocular allusion to the late George's pleasure at having a pretty girl sit on his lap. The suicide motif is also important for two less obvious reasons: First, self-murder is one of the traditional means of becoming a vampire; second, after Mina becomes Dracula's victim, she considers killing herself, and Van Helsing vehemently warns her against the act (chapter 22). The tale of George also functions subliminally, perhaps, to undercut Dracula's satanic grandeur by associating the vampire lord with a sordid history of domestic hatred. Lucy's distress at being made to face the facts about George (as opposed to the lies on the tombstone) and reinterpret a story she had assumed she understood adumbrates the radical dissonance between her interpretation of her own life-story and the way that story in fact unfolds.

Swales constantly dwells upon the Last Judgment and the "hope of a glorious resurrection"—a phrase that gains new resonance when we find Lucy undergoing a diabolical resurrection after being transformed into a vampire. Dracula-as-Antichrist is one of the story's major themes, and some of his actions explicitly parody Christian mysteries, as we shall consider below. When Swales reassures Lucy and Mina that they need not fear the peaceful dead, he adds, "It'll be time for ye to be getting scart when ye see the tombsteans all run away with" (*Dracula,* 70). Foreshadowed here is the terror that Lucy's friends will suffer when the dead literally begin to leave their tombs. A few days later Swales repents of his outspoken skepticism, which he attributes to his own fear of death, for he is nearly a century old. Longevity is another of the novel's motifs, emphasized in Van Helsing's lecture on the mysteries of life in chapter 14. Dracula, like Melmoth and Margrave, offers an unnatural prolongation of life, preserving the body at the expense of the soul. Swales, perhaps, would be tempted by this offer, but his repentance presumably saves him, freeing him to resign himself to relinquishing his long-held mortal life. He tells Lucy and Mina that he feels a premonition of his approaching death, and he does in fact die a few nights later—of shock, at the sight of Dracula. Somewhat like Renfield, though unwittingly, Swales is a prophet, a harbinger of Dracula's advent, and he turns out to be the vampire's first English "victim." The old man's palinode looks forward to the manner of Lucy's facing death in chapter 12; she is at first rebellious, but at last piously submissive. (And once again belief or disbelief in the supernatural is linked to faith in God.) Immediately after Swales' farewell to the heroines, the ship bearing the vampire Count washes ashore at Whitby during a storm.

The "tedious" chapters of *Dracula,* then, employ techniques of gossip and secondhand narrative to prepare our minds, in a commonplace, humdrum setting, for the shocking events to come. They also cast doubt on the reliability of all the pieces of testimony that combine to make up the novel. If seemingly trivial and nonessential narratives turn out to be problematic, narratives of critical events are also open to suspicion. The testimony of the principal characters is further placed in doubt by the continual questioning of their mental balance.

Senf mentions, in her paragraph on the prevalence of insanity in *Dracula,* Stoker's hints of madness with reference to Lucy's "schizophrenia" (by which Senf means something like "multiple personality"), Dr. Seward's self-doubt, and Jonathan's nervous breakdown (Senf, 162–63). But she does not go far enough. In addition to the lunatic Renfield (whose madness carries its own ambiguities), almost every participant in the action—even Dracula himself—has his sanity questioned at least once. While some of these suggestions of instability are perfunctory or merely figurative, they still contribute to the dominant imagery of madness; moreover, several of these doubts are seriously entertained. Jonathan, for instance, is certainly out of his mind for a period; the question tormenting him is whether the insanity generated delusions of vampirism or whether the vampiric experience is real and caused the insanity. Dr. Seward broods at some length over his own disquieting resemblances to Renfield.

A compulsive rationalist, Seward, director of a London sanitorium, doubts not only his own mental health, but that of his all-wise teacher, Van Helsing. In the bizarre "King Laugh" scene (chapter 13), Van Helsing is accused of "nervous . . . weakness" (*Dracula,* 158); when the Professor unfolds suspicions of vampirism after Lucy's death, Seward goes so far as to ask: "I wonder if his mind can have become in any way unhinged. . . . He is so abnormally clever that if he went off his head he would carry out his intent with regard to some fixed idea in a wonderful way. . . . Indeed it would be almost as great a marvel . . . to find that Van Helsing was mad" (*Dracula,* 184). (Clearly Stoker is exploiting the notion of genius' kinship with insanity.) The young doctor, though, is harder on himself than on anyone else. Seward compares himself to the mad Renfield on the ground that Seward too is susceptible to the temptation of "fixed ideas . . . for may not I too be of an exceptional brain, congenitally?" Later he wonders "if my long habit of life amongst the insane is beginning to tell on my own brain" (*Dracula*, 74, 127). As a student of the mind, he is aware of the frailty of the door between the madman's cell and the real world.

In *Dracula* the world on the "sane" side of the bars abounds in hints of insanity. Images of derangement cluster in the background of the picture. Van Helsing's own wife has long been confined to an asylum (a gratuitous touch of horror—and surely a kind of death in life). Lucy's father was a habitual sleepwalker, hence assumed by some nineteenth-century beliefs to be suffering from a form of brain abnormality (*Dracula*, 74-75). Lucy, inheriting this nervous weakness, succumbs to it long before Dracula claims her.* Her deterioration accelerates under the vampire's influence, until Seward, upon reading Lucy's account of Dracula's final assault, is moved to exclaim, "Was she, or is she, mad?" Most chilling is Lucy's earlier comparison of herself to "Ophelia in the play, with 'virgin crants and maiden strewments'" (*Dracula*, 139, 125). Aside from the fact that Ophelia is dead on her bier in the scene alluded to, the heroine of *Hamlet* is, of course, best known for her madness.

Other minds are deranged by Dracula's touch. The *Demeter* loses her entire complement to the vampire, and her captain originally believes that the first mate, gone mad, is responsible for the disappearances. The captain (as noted above) is suspected, after death, of having lost his reason and committed the murders. In England Lucy's fiancé, Arthur, is shaken by the vampire's influence; when Van Helsing reveals that Lucy is an Undead, Arthur exclaims, "Are you mad that speak such things, or am I mad to listen to them?" Even the strong-willed Mina succumbs to self-doubt when Dracula's glowing mist invades her chamber. At first she thinks she is experiencing a sort of vision, but fear supersedes awe, and she tells herself, "I must be careful of such dreams, for they would unseat one's reason if there were too much of them" (*Dracula*, 186, 230). While the cross keeps the vampire's spiritual corruption at bay, there seems no adequate defense against his insidious attack on the mind.

It is Renfield who bears the full fury of this attack. Yet the lunatic Renfield is a paradox, of whom Van Helsing says, "Perhaps I may gain more knowledge out of the folly of this madman than I shall from the teaching of the most wise" (*Dracula*, 227). Renfield turns out to be sanest when immersed in the lurid fantasy of vampirism. (Or so we must assume—for we cannot evade the irony that all our knowledge of how Dracula gains entry to the house where Mina is sheltered rests on the lunatic's testimony.) Only then does he rise above his derangement to become "a sane man fighting for his soul." Only

---

*We are reminded of Poe's "Berenice," with its somnambulistic hero and cataleptic heroine. Vampiric elements are evident in Berenice's return from death and the protagonist's obsession with her teeth, culminating in his desecration of her grave.

when he begs to be sent away for Mina's safety, ironically, do Seward and Van Helsing finally reject him as incurably mad (chapter 18). Here Renfield is "the sanest lunatic," Seward obstinately blind to reality, and Van Helsing an "old fool" (*Dracula,* 219, 220, 227). Despite this rejection Renfield sacrifices himself in Mina's defense, dying sane.

Dracula, strangely enough, is compared to Renfield. The vampire, says Van Helsing, is "more prisoner than . . . the madman in his cell" (*Dracula,* 213). Van Helsing sometimes departs from his usual religious vocabulary to treat the Count's evil as a psychological aberration conforming to the scientific criminology of Nordau and Lombroso (chapter 25). In Stoker's novel, in fact, the whole world is figuratively implicated in madness—a pandemic insanity made explicit by Van Helsing when he cautions Seward to discretion: Just as the doctor conceals his true thoughts from his mental patients, so he must conceal the full truth from "God's madmen—the rest of the world." Seward, once more, sums up these implications when he says, "I sometimes think we must all be mad and that we shall wake to sanity in strait-waistcoats" (*Dracula,* 115, 242). Ever since Poe, the convention of opening a fantastic tale with some sentence like, "They say I am mad," has become a cliché. Stoker's strategy of casting doubt on the sanity of all the principal characters of a full-length novel is possibly unique. But how thoroughly is the cognitive dissonance inflicted on the characters by the vampire's invasion of their mundane lives transmitted to the reader? In *Dracula* the implied reader stands, compared to the characters, in a privileged position. When Jonathan's "brain fever" has made him forget his ordeal in Castle Dracula, we as readers remember the contents of the journal. We recall the incredible experiences presented in the opening chapters as (in Jonathan's perception) objective fact. This memory guides our interpretation of later documents such as the *Demeter*'s log and the interview with the zookeeper. We enjoy a comprehensive knowledge of all the testimony relevant to Dracula's invasion of England, while the characters—until Mina produces her "mass of type-writing" (*Dracula,* 332)—are restricted to fragmented reports. Their uncertainty can be resolved only by joining and collating these fragments.

All these techniques help to maintain an atmosphere of doubt, of hesitation between natural and supernatural views of reality. *Dracula* remains a story of the fantastic until the last few chapters, only then moving into the realm of the marvelous, the supernatural accepted as real. The epilogue, however, reasserts doubt and plunges us back into the world of the fantastic. At this point, in the final words of the novel, Van Helsing, who introduced the vampire hypothesis and has held to it unshakably, abandons the search for evidential proof and advances no rational defense for his world view; acceptance of the supernatural at last rests only on faith, grounded in personal experience. He says with reference to Jonathan and Mina's son: "We want no proofs; we ask none to believe us! This boy will some day know what a brave and gallant woman his mother is. Already he knows her sweetness and loving care; later on he will understand how some men so loved her, that they did dare much for her sake" (*Dracula,* 332). This summation, we note, stands at a seven-year remove from the body of the tale—a seemingly gratuitous bit of distancing. As Jonathan says, a "mass of material" containing "hardly one authentic document" is insufficient evidence for "so wild a story" (*Dracula,* 332). Faith in the unseen world, based on direct experience of the power of love, takes the place of proof.

Are proof and faith in fact antithetical? Orthodox Christianity might say so. As C. S. Lewis puts it, regarding belief in God, "the ambiguity is not something that conflicts with faith so much as a condition that makes faith possible. . . . There would be no room for trust if demonstration were given" (Lewis, "On Obstinacy in Belief," 28). Once having obtained incontrovertible proof, we do not speak of faith, but of knowledge. In *Dracula,* more than in any other work we have examined (except, perhaps, *A Strange Story*), belief in supernatural evil is bound up with faith in God. The motif of Dracula-as-Antichrist entails the existence of the Divine Adversary. Van Helsing, presented as a devout Roman Catholic, is the character who constantly draws our attention to this facet of the vampire's nature. Catholicism, a symbol of rampant superstition in the eighteenth-century Gothic, serves a different function here. Radcliffe's characters, we recall, face the task of finding the mean between superstition and skepticism; the Roman Catholic Church offers one convenient image of the former extreme. In the nineteenth century (as we have seen in connection with Lytton) materialism as a threat so far overshadows superstition that Catholicism need not be used in this way. Jonathan, indeed, harks back to the traditional Protestant-rationalist view when, being offered a crucifix, he reflects, "I did not know what to do, for, as an English Churchman, I have been taught to regard such things as in some measure idolatrous" (*Dracula,* 7). Stoker however does not endorse this attitude (as Radcliffe would); he presents the dominant scientific rationalism of his day as deficient on this point. Subsequent events prove the "superstitious" and "idolatrous" object to be Jonathan's only defense against the danger of which the Transylvanian peasants vainly warn him in the words "'Ordog'—Satan, 'pokol'—hell" (*Dracula,* 7).

Though the vampire is identified with Satan from the first, it is Van Helsing who unfolds the full implications of this identity. When Jonathan calls Transylvania "this cursed land, where the devil and his children still walk with earthly feet," he may be speaking metaphorically. It is less likely that Van Helsing is doing so in Lucy's sickroom when he exclaims, "How are all the powers of the devils against us!" (*Dracula,* 55, 127). The solemnity of his belief that opposing Dracula means fighting for God is first conveyed to the other characters by the Professor's use of the Eucharistic wafer to seal Lucy's tomb. Seward says that this action "appalled the most sceptical of us" (*Dracula,* 189). It is unclear whether the skepticism mentioned is directed only toward vampires or toward the spiritual world in general. Van Helsing defines the vampire fighters' mission in exalted terms reminiscent of medieval romance:

> Thus are we ministers of God's own wish: that the world, and men for whom His Son die, will not be given over to monsters, whose very existence would defame Him. He have allowed us to redeem one soul already, and we go out as the old knights of the Cross to redeem more. Like them we shall travel towards the sunrise; and like them, if we fall, we fall in good cause. (*Dracula,* 282)

(The grammatical irregularities in Van Helsing's speech represent Stoker's idea of a Dutch accent.) Though the heroes continually express submission to God's will and trust in His protection, the outcome of their crusade is far from certain. Eternal as well as bodily life can be lost to the vampire; we recall that Renfield fights for his soul, not only his mind. Until a vampire is granted the true death, his or her soul is enslaved, "working wickedness by night and growing more debased in the assimilation of it by day," and he or she is "a blot on the face of God's sunshine," to whom "for ever are the gates of heaven shut" (*Dracula,* 193, 211). In the war against this evil, martyrdom can be achieved. Renfield and Quincey Morris die martyrs' deaths, especially the latter, who sacrifices himself for Mina's sake and is revered almost as a saint by his surviving friends. Of Mina herself it is explicitly said at one point that "her eyes shone with the devotion of a martyr" (*Dracula,* 258). Though preserved from physical death, she persuades her friends to read the service for burial of the dead over her (chapter 25). She bears, moreover, an ambiguous brand inflicted by a holy wafer applied to her forehead in an attempt to protect her. This mark represents a taint of uncleanness resulting from Dracula's predation (being, in fact, a duplicate of a scar on Dracula's own brow). It recalls, moreover, the diabolical immortality of the Wandering Jew, marked like Cain—perhaps an echo of *Melmoth.* Yet it also seems a visible sign of Mina's participation in the passion of Christ, like the stigmata of a saint:

> For so surely as we live, that scar shall pass away when God sees right to lift the burden that is hard upon us. Till then we bear our Cross, as His Son did in obedience to His will. It may be that we are chosen instruments of His good pleasure, and that we ascend to His bidding as that other through stripes and shame; through tears and blood. (*Dracula,* 263)

These passages and many similar ones illustrate the link between belief in vampirism and belief in God postulated in *Dracula.* At one point Van Helsing even makes the connection explicit: "And to superstition must we trust at the first; it was man's faith in the early [sic], and it have its root in faith still" (*Dracula,* 288).

The connection is so tight that the novel could be read as falling into dualism. If the vampire can even damn souls of otherwise innocent victims, he must be operating independent of Divine permission. (Mina, though the purity of her heart is continually stressed, is still tainted.) We find ourselves in a Manichean world where Evil seems to be as self-existent as Good. Dracula is presented, not merely as an avatar of Satan, but as an Antichrist and even Anti-God. The mad Renfield worships Dracula as Lord and Master, serving and praying to the vampire. The lunatic says of his own role, "I am, so far as concerns things purely terrestrial, somewhat in the position which Enoch occupied spiritually!" Just as Enoch walked with God, Renfield walks with the Lord of this world, Dracula/Satan. Dracula imitates the creative act of God the Father in his ambition to become "father or furtherer of a new order of beings, whose road must lead through Death, not Life" (*Dracula,* 238, 268). How the vampire's rising from the grave parodies the Christian resurrection of the body is obvious. The follower of Christ must lose his life in order to find it (Matthew 10:39), and after death he expects to rise again to a transfigured existence; in St. Paul's words, "It is sown a physical body, it is raised a spiritual body" (I Corinthians 15:44). The vampire attempts to circumvent this process, bestowing an immortality not spiritual but physical, subhuman rather than superhuman. The vampire also parodies the sacraments. Renfield's biblical quotation upon his first taste of blood, "The blood is the life!," suggests Holy Communion, as does the telepathic union of minds between Dracula and Mina after he forces her to drink his blood. This ritual is called by Van Helsing "the Vampire's baptism of blood." The mutual sharing of blood also parodies the sacrament of marriage, as indicated by Dracula's boast, "And you... are now to me, flesh of my flesh; blood of my blood; kin of my kin" (*Dracula,* 133, 284, 255).

The antithetical connection between the Divine and the diabolical sometimes threatens to become, strangely enough, conflation or identification. Mina, when she first sees Dracula invading her room in the form of mist, is reminded of the pillar of cloud and fire that guided the Exodus; she wonders if the vision is a form of "spiritual guidance" (*Dracula,* 229). In view of Van Helsing's insistence on Dracula's diabolical nature, it is a shock to find the vampire momentarily mistaken for his opposite. (So, we recall, is Melmoth, with his deceptive "celestial music.") Yet the paradox thus suggested is expressly stated in other contexts. The vampire can rest only on a bed of his native earth, and it must be, moreover, consecrated earth. Van Helsing says of Dracula: "There have been from the loins of this very one great men and good women, and their graves make sacred the earth where alone this foulness can dwell. For it is not the least of its terrors that this evil thing is rooted deep in all good; in soil barren of holy memories it cannot rest" (*Dracula,* 214). This statement might rescue the novel from the charge of dualism, since an evil "rooted deep in all good" conforms to the Christian doctrine of evil as derivative and parasitic. On the other hand, the image of tangled interdependence between good and evil might be considered even more heterodox. The confusion is far from relieved by Van Helsing's plan to sterilize Dracula's native earth with the Host in order to "defeat him with his own weapon" by making the consecrated soil "more holy still" (*Dracula,* 264). How this process works is not explained. The entire mystery remains unassimilated and yet, unlike the question of madness, seems to stimulate no dissonance in the characters' minds. Leonard Wolf's idea that these passages are intended to suggest hope for Dracula's eventual salvation (Wolf, *Dracula,* 215) is supported by Van Helsing's remark, "Oh! if such an one was to come from God, and not the Devil, what a force for good might he not be in this old world of ours" (Wolf, 282). This remark may be only a reference to the corruption of Dracula's originally noble nature (like Lucifer's), or it may be a hint, never repeated, that vampiric powers after all might be morally neutral, capable of serving either good or evil.*

Alongside the novel's religious theme runs an incompatible theme, apparently not recognized as such by the characters, of an amoral force, natural or preternatural. When Van Helsing rages, "Is there fate amongst us still, sent down from the pagan world of old, that such things must be, and in such way?" (*Dracula,* 127), he momentarily steps outside the Christian world into a realm of blind power. The mysteries upon which he lectures to Seward in chapter 14 seem similarly unrelated to Divine Providence. He urges Seward to keep an open mind toward inexplicable phenomena: "Do you not think that there are things which you cannot understand, and yet which are; that some people see things that others cannot?" (*Dracula,* 172). In this passage the science that so preoccupies the two doctors through most of the book is castigated for its narrow-mindedness. Instead mystery is celebrated, especially the mysteries of longevity:

> Why was it that Methuselah lived nine hundred years, and "Old Parr" one hundred and sixty-nine, and yet that poor Lucy, with four men's blood in her poor veins, could not live even one day? . . . Can you tell me why, when other spiders die small and soon, that one great

---

*Carol Senf goes even further, asserting a moral "similarity between vampire and opponents" and insisting that the heroes' "commitment to social values merely masks their violence and their sexuality" (Senf, 167). The good/evil opposition between Dracula and his pursuers, in other words, might plausibly be reversed. Dracula, after all, is not allowed to defend himself. We get no unmediated access to his mind, no document from his hand except a short note transcribed into Jonathan's journal.

spider lived for centuries in the tower of the old Spanish church and grew and grew, till, on descending, he could drink the oil of all the church lamps?...Can you tell me why the tortoise lives more long than generations of men; why the elephant goes on and on till he have seen dynasties; and why the parrot never die only of bite of cat or dog or other complaint? (*Dracula*, 73–74)

These phenomena are presented as morally neutral, including the spider, which might ordinarily be considered monstrous (another merely physical parody of spiritual immortality, significantly occurring in a church), and later the Indian fakir who has himself buried and rises to life again months afterward. In chapter 24 Van Helsing unexpectedly attributes Dracula's powers to the way "all the forces of nature that are occult and deep and strong must have worked together in some wondrous way" amid the strange ecology of the Count's homeland (*Dracula*, 281). Stoker makes no attempt to reconcile the imagery of an amoral natural force with the religious imagery, nor do the characters remark on the discrepancy. The reader, however, is left with an impression of cognitive dissonance invading the realm of value as well as the realm of fact. The novel, as we have seen, hesitates between natural and supernatural explanations of events (i.e., between the hypotheses of illness—physical and mental—and vampirism), but also between religious and irreligious evaluations of those events. Though the weight of the novel falls on the side of the Christian world view, suggestions of a struggle between unaided mortals and some incomprehensible, amoral power coexist uneasily with this view. We discover that in *Dracula* the discourse of the fantastic generates at least two kinds of ambiguity: for the characters, uncertainty whether their sufferings are due to vampirism or to natural illness complicated by delusion; and for the reader, uncertainty about the metaphysical and moral status of the vampire.

Conclusion

This study has examined a selection of Gothic romances and tales from a one-hundred-year period in English literature, from the late eighteenth century to the late nineteenth. I have tried to show a relationship between mediated narrative in this fiction and certain attitudes toward the supposed supernatural. In demonstrating this relationship we have had to take note of various influences upon the development of narrative fiction in the seventeenth and eighteenth centuries and the impact of scientific discoveries upon such fiction in the nineteenth.

The novelist's decision to tell a story through multiple voices or to filter the main narrator's voice through one or more frames impels consideration of the validity of testimony. How can a witness' reliability be judged? If his statement comes to us at second- or third-hand, how do we evaluate those who vouch for him? In the eighteenth century these questions are connected with the new philosophy's impact on changing standards of legal, scientific, and theological proof. It is no surprise that prose fiction also grapples with these concerns. The witnesses in our texts are challenged with regard to their factual and moral judgments of supernatural or preternatural events. These characters' ambiguous perceptions often foreground the clash between a spiritual and purely material view of reality. While in the eighteenth century the conflict centers on the new philosophy (with its distrust for the nonrational) in general, nineteenth-century fiction of the supernatural is more apt to focus on the challenge posed by new discoveries in the physical sciences. Though the characters' responses are always (at least initially and sometimes throughout) ambiguous, the degree of doubt exhibited by the implied author varies widely. He may take an authoritative stance, strongly prescribing the reader's response to the variety of testimony presented, or at the other extreme he may make himself invisible.

Our authors are ranged at various points on the continuum bounded by these polarities. The two German authors, Maturin, and Lytton state their explicit messages in "editorial" prefaces, the last two using footnotes as well. Maturin's interpolated narratives, however, tend to undercut the author's stated position. In Lytton, the most overtly didactic of the group, we find the greatest harmony between the author's explicit aim and the text's implications. Radcliffe, rather than resorting to prefatory statements of purpose, conveys her attitude toward her characters' actions and beliefs by more indirect means, such as using respected figures within the narrative as her spokesmen. Le Fanu and Stoker, on the other hand, offer no overt authorial guidance at all. In their fiction the reader, confronted with a collection of material, must devise his own interpretation. Is it coincidental that both of these fall late in our period? Perhaps in their fiction the late Victorian crisis in belief is reflected in an unwillingness to make a positive statement about the nature of reality. We are reminded of Wayne Booth's observation that in fiction generally, the closer we approach our own literary contemporaries, the more often we encounter unreliable narrators and ambiguous effects. "Direct and authoritative rhetoric," as Booth says, "is not what we are likely to find if we turn to a typical modern novel or short story" (Booth, 6). We have also discovered a contrast between novels suspicious of belief in the supernatural (those of Radcliffe and the Germans) and those that actually promote this belief (notably Lytton). Again, Lytton's championship of a spiritual view of reality and Stoker's invocation of supernatural mysteries belong to a later period than Radcliffe's rationalism. Perhaps by the second half of the nineteenth century materialism has come to be perceived as a graver threat than superstition.

Moving from the nineteenth to the twentieth century (beyond the scope of this study), we find the marvelous becoming more prevalent than the pure fantastic in supernatural fiction. In both marvelous and fantastic fiction the familiar world appears to be invaded by something other. But in the former case the focus is often less on the invader, and its problematic status, than on ordinary people's reaction to the invasion. For the average twentieth-century reader, the supernatural is not problematic; it is apt to be rejected without debate. The eighteenth and nineteenth centuries held no uncontestably dominant consensus on these matters, whether of acceptance or rejection. Tales of the supernatural in this period are addressed to the skeptic or agnostic, whose acceptance of the supernatural cannot be assumed, and employ a rhetoric of skepticism congenial to such a reader. Our readings have shown that mediated narrative in such fiction highlights the isolation, alienation, and moral ambiguities experienced by characters uncertain of how to interpret their own apparently supernatural experiences. The reader, for the duration of the narrative, is invited to share the characters' doubt, and in texts where the ostensibly authoritative editor appears unreliable, the implied reader must remain in a condition of radical uncertainty. We have also discovered how, in each era, these concerns embodied in tales of supernatural horror grow out of the philosophic preoccupations of society as a whole.

However the uses of the supernatural vary with the needs of each era, William Patrick Day's summary remains valid: "The content of the Gothic fantasy lies, finally, in the interaction between the assumptions and expectations of its audience with the fears and anxieties produced by those assumptions and expectations and in the way it treats conventional versions of reality and identity, as well as fear and anxiety" (Day, 13). A primary function of the Gothic is to place the reader's world view in question.

There are numerous other works that could have found a place in this study. We have passed over two eminent nineteenth-century instances of narrative doubt applied to the putative supernatural, "The Fall of the House of Usher" and *The Turn of the Screw,* since as American works they fall outside the limits set for this study. In these two tales, Poe and James, respectively, invite the reader to hesitate between interpreting events in terms of the supernatural or of madness, and in each case the "facts" are filtered through a narrator of questionable reliability. James, in addition, employs a distancing narrative frame. Nor does our own century lack examples of such fiction. We might mention H. P. Lovecraft, whose tales focus on the theme of the incommunicable secret and sometimes use multiple narrators as a vehicle. His "Call of Cthulhu," a story constructed from a collection of documents, conveys the message that their collation is an ill-conceived act, that lifting the veil between our world and any other produces only despair. In Lovecraft's "The Thing on the Doorstep" the reader is at the mercy of a single first-person narrator, one who (like many of Poe's protagonists) lies under suspicion of madness and has, moreover, obtained most of his information from a supposed madman. Theodore Sturgeon's novel *Some of Your Blood,* though not seriously suggesting a supernatural origin for its monster's crimes, does use the documentary form to rationalize a contemporary vampire. The reader is invited to open an Army psychiatrist's file drawer and pass judgment on the vampire. But Sturgeon, by thus involving the reader, implicates him in the patient's evil or madness; by judging, the reader does not elevate himself (like a Radcliffean reader) but incriminates himself. In the recent novel *Ghost Story* Peter Straub uses multiple points of view and layers of retrospective narration to portray a ghost whose nature is never quite clear and whose counter-charges against the heroes cannot be quite disproved. This story, like Sturgeon's, implies that evil must be confronted within as well as without the self. For these authors (unlike Radcliffe, whose suggestions of the supernatural work ultimately to reassure the reader) lifting the veil becomes a hazardous project, perhaps better avoided. If supernatural fiction's typical conflict grows out of the new philosophy in the eighteenth century and the physical sciences in the nineteenth, in the twentieth it tends to focus on the science of the mind, carrying Stoker's theme of self-doubt to new lengths.

Among contemporary writers, however, the pure fantastic seems to be outweighed by the marvelous. The field of nineteenth-century fiction contains a plethora of fantastic tales from which to choose the few I have discussed. To present twentieth-century examples, I had to hunt slightly harder. Do we find, typically, any difference in function between supernatural tales written in the fantastic mode and those written in the marvelous mode? A characteristic modern instance of the latter is the work of Stephen King. In King's novels of supernatural horror (e.g., *Carrie, 'Salem's Lot, The Shining, Christine, Pet Sematary, Thinner, It*) the marvelous element is introduced early and is never seriously doubted, even by the protagonist (much less the reader, with his advantage of generic expectations). The hero of *Pet Sematary*, for instance, tries to concoct a natural explanation for his cat's apparent return from the grave, but he knows he is grasping at straws and never for a moment believes his own explanation—in contrast to the never-resolved doubts of Poe's narrator in "The Black Cat." In keeping with our observations about the structures of fantastic and marvelous fiction, King's novels are almost always told by an omniscient narrator. *Carrie*, in which this narrator also introduces some fragments of documentary evidence, is not quite pure fantasy, lying on the border of science fiction. *Christine*, the exception among King's purely supernatural novels, resembles *Bleak House* in being conveyed partly by the omniscient narrator and partly by the hero in first person. The tales contain little temporal dislocation, and that which does appear is usually confined to a character's private recollections.

We know from King's own utterances, in his nonfictional *Danse Macabre* and other sources, that he conceives an alethetic function for supernatural horror: to confront and exorcise our emotions concerning the mysteries of existence, particularly the mystery of death. But the subtext of the novels mentioned does not seem to aim at altering the reader's attitude toward the supernatural realm as such. In these cases of the familiar world's invasion by something other, the focus is not so much on the invader itself as on ordinary people's reaction to the invasion. The marvelous element in the tale is used to draw our attention to some human response the author wishes to illuminate. Clayton Koelb asserts that although not all allegories are alethetic fictions, "*all* alethetic fictions may be called allegories" (Koelb, 33). King's supernatural novels often feature strong overtones of allegory. *Carrie*, for example, is not "about" telekinesis so much as it is "about" the male fear of the female's secret power. *Pet Sematary* uses demonic resurrection to comment on the futility of attempting to deny or evade the ineluctable fact of death. *Thinner* uses a Gypsy curse to highlight the self-centeredness of the affluent American, as expressed by an obsession with body weight.

I suspect that when the supernatural element of a story is a *donnée*, rather than the focus of debate and speculation (as in the fantastic mode), it is often used in a quasi-allegorical way. Perhaps most twentieth-century fantasists assume that the supernatural—at least, the "lower" supernatural—is not a live option for their readers and therefore see no reason to use it as a focus for ambiguity. Instead, the supernatural furnishes an excellent framework for a moral fable, since there is no danger of confusing the story's incredible literal level with the truths of its figurative level. The pure marvelous was common in medieval romance because that culture's univocal consensus accepted the supernatural as fact; perhaps the marvelous is common in modern romance for the opposite reason—the author assumes a consensus that accepts the absence of the supernatural as fact.

Our texts illustrate how an author's position on the supernatural can be related to his overall world view and how he can use Gothic fiction to dramatize either the concurrence or the disagreement of that world view with the dominant culture's. We have also seen how an author's use of multiple narrators and mediated narrative can place the ultimate burden of interpretation, with or without the direct guidance of the author-within-the-text, on the reader—that is, on each of us.

Bibliography

Primary

Boswell, James. *Life of Johnson,* ed. R. W. Chapman. London: Oxford University Press, 1970.
Fielding, Henry. "Examples of the Interposition of Providence in the Detection and Punishment of Murder." In *The Works of Henry Fielding,* vols. 1–16. New York: Barnes and Noble, 1967.
_____. *Tom Jones.* New York: Random House, 1950.
Flammenberg, Lawrence. *The Necromancer, or The Tale of the Black Forest,* trans. Peter Teuthold, ed. D. P. Varma. London: Folio Press, 1968.
Grosse, Karl. *Horrid Mysteries,* trans. Peter Will, ed. D. P. Varma. London: Folio Press, 1968.
Hume, David. *Dialogues Concerning Natural Religion,* ed. Henry D. Aiken. New York: Hafner, 1966.
_____. *A Treatise of Human Nature,* ed. L. A. Selby-Bigge. London: Oxford University Press, 1888.
Hurd, Richard. "Letters on Chivalry and Romance." In *The Works of Richard Hurd, D. D., Lord Bishop of Winchester,* vols. 1–8, 1811. New York: Arno Press, 1967.
Le Fanu, J. S. *Best Ghost Stories of J. S. Le Fanu,* ed. E. F. Bleiler. New York: Dover, 1964.
Lewis, Matthew G. *The Monk,* ed. Louis F. Peck. New York: Grove Press, 1952.
Lytton, Sir Edward Bulwer. *A Strange Story and The Haunted and the Haunters,* 1862. Philadelphia: J. B. Lippincott, 1875.
Maturin, Charles Robert. *Melmoth the Wanderer.* Lincoln: University of Nebraska Press, 1961.
Radcliffe, Ann. *Gaston de Blondeville,* ed. D. P. Varma. New York: Arno Press, 1972.
_____. *The Italian,* ed. D. P. Varma. New York: Russell and Russell, 1968.
_____. *The Mysteries of Udolpho,* ed. Bonamy Dobree. London: Oxford University Press, 1970.
_____. *A Sicilian Romance,* ed. D. P. Varma. New York: Arno Press, 1972.
Shelley, Mary. *Frankenstein, or The Modern Prometheus,* intro. Robert E. Dowse and D. J. Palmer. London: J. M. Dent, 1963.
Stoker, Bram. *The Annotated Dracula,* ed. Leonard Wolf. New York: Clarkson N. Potter, 1975.
Walpole, Horace. *The Castle of Otranto,* ed. W. S. Lewis. Oxford: Oxford University Press, 1982.

Secondary

Books

Auerbach, Nina. *Woman and the Demon: The Life of a Victorian Myth.* Cambridge: Harvard University Press, 1982.
Baine, Rodney M. *Daniel Defoe and the Supernatural.* Athens: University of Georgia Press, 1968.

Bloom, Harold. *The Anxiety of Influence: A Theory of Poetry.* New York: Oxford University Press, 1973.

Booth, Wayne. *The Rhetoric of Fiction.* Chicago: University of Chicago Press, 1961.

Boucher, Anthony. "Introduction." In Bram Stoker, *Dracula.* New York: George Macy, 1965.

Braudy, Leo. *Narrative Form in History and Fiction.* Princeton: Princeton University Press, 1970.

Brooks, Peter. *Reading for the Plot: Design and Intention in Narrative.* New York: Knopf, 1984.

Buckley, Jerome Hamilton. *The Victorian Temper: A Study in Literary Culture,* 1951. New York: Random House, n.d.

Cassirer, Ernst. *The Philosophy of the Enlightenment,* trans. Fritz C. A. Koellin and James P. Pettegrove, 1951. Boston: Beacon Press, 1955.

Chandler, Alice. *A Dream of Order: The Medieval Ideal in Nineteenth-Century English Literature.* Lincoln: University of Nebraska Press, 1970.

Chapman, Raymond. *The Victorian Debate: English Literature and Society, 1832–1901.* New York: Basic Books, 1968.

Day, Robert Adams. *Told in Letters: Epistolary Fiction before Richardson.* Ann Arbor: University of Michigan Press, 1966.

Day, William Patrick. *In the Circles of Fear and Desire: A Study of Gothic Fantasy.* Chicago: University of Chicago Press, 1985.

Eigner, Edwin M. *The Metaphysical Novel in England and America.* Berkeley: University of California Press, 1978.

Foucault, Michel. *Madness and Civilization: A History of Insanity in the Age of Reason,* trans. Richard Howard. New York: Random House, 1965.

Freud, Sigmund. "The 'Uncanny.'" In *The Standard Edition of the Complete Psychological Works of Sigmund Freud,* ed. James Strachey, 24 vols. London: Hogarth Press, 1955.

Frye, Northrop. *A Study of English Romanticism.* New York: Random House, 1968.

Gilbert, Sandra M., and Susan Gubar. *The Madwoman in the Attic: The Woman Writer and the Nineteenth-Century Literary Imagination.* New Haven, Conn.: Yale University Press, 1979.

Gose, Elliott B. *Imagination Indulged: The Irrational in the Nineteenth-Century Novel.* Montreal: McGill-Queen's University Press, 1972.

Hanning, Robert W. *The Individual in Twelfth-Century Romance.* New Haven, Conn.: Yale University Press, 1977.

Hartman, Geoffrey H. "False Themes and Gentle Minds." In *Beyond Formalism: Literary Essays, 1958–1970.* New Haven, Conn.: Yale University Press, 1970.

Hofstadter, Richard. "The Paranoid Style in American Politics." In *The Paranoid Style in American Politics and Other Essays.* New York: Knopf, 1965.

Houghton, Walter E. *The Victorian Frame of Mind, 1830–1870.* New Haven, Conn.: Yale University Press, 1957.

Hume, Robert D. "Exuberant Gloom, Existential Agony, and Heroic Despair: Three Varieties of Negative Romanticism." In G. R. Thompson, ed., *The Gothic Imagination: Essays in Dark Romanticism,* pp. 109–27. Pullman: Washington State University Press, 1974.

Hunter, J. Paul. *The Reluctant Pilgrim: Defoe's Emblematic Method and Quest for Form in Robinson Crusoe.* Baltimore, Md.: Johns Hopkins University Press, 1966.

Iser, Wolfgang. *The Implied Reader: Patterns of Communication in Prose Fiction from Bunyan to Beckett.* Baltimore, Md.: Johns Hopkins University Press, 1974.

Jackson, Rosemary. *Fantasy: The Literature of Subversion.* New York: Methuen, 1981.

Johnston, Arthur. *Enchanted Ground: The Study of Medieval Romance in the Eighteenth Century.* London: University of London, the Athlone Press, 1964.

Kincaid, Juliet Willman. "The Novel as Journal: A Generic Study." Dissertation. Columbus: Ohio State University, 1977.

Koelb, Clayton. *The Incredulous Reader: Literature and the Function of Disbelief.* Ithaca, N.Y.: Cornell University Press, 1984.

Korshin, Paul J. *Typologies in England: 1650–1820.* Princeton, N.J.: Princeton University Press, 1982.

Levine, George, and U. C. Knoepflmacher, eds. *The Endurance of* Frankenstein. Berkeley: University of California Press, 1979.

Lewis, C. S. "On Obstinacy in Belief." In *The World's Last Night and Other Essays.* New York: Harcourt, Brace, 1960.

Lovecraft, H. P. *Supernatural Horror in Literature,* 1945. New York: Dover, 1973.

Lovejoy, Arthur O. *Essays in the History of Ideas.* Baltimore, Md.: Johns Hopkins University Press, 1948.

MacAndrew, Elizabeth. *The Gothic Tradition in Fiction.* New York: Columbia University Press, 1979.

McIntyre, Clara Frances. *Ann Radcliffe in Relation to Her Time,* 1920. Hamden, Conn.: Archon Books, 1970.

Manlove, C. M. *Modern Fantasy: Five Studies.* Cambridge: Cambridge University Press, 1975.

Newsom, Robert. *Dickens on the Romantic Side of Familiar Things:* Bleak House *and the Novel Tradition.* New York: Columbia University Press, 1977.

Peavoy, John Roger. "Artificial Terrors and Real Horrors: The Supernatural in Gothic Fiction." Dissertation. Waltham, Mass.: Brandeis University, 1980.

Porte, Joel. "In the Hands of an Angry God: Religious Terror in Gothic Fiction." In G. R. Thompson, ed., *The Gothic Imagination: Essays in Dark Romanticism,* pp. 42–64. Pullman: Washington State University Press, 1974.

Preston, Thomas R. *Not in Timon's Manner: Feeling, Misanthropy, and Satire in Eighteenth-Century England.* University: University of Alabama Press, 1975.

Schacht, Richard. *Alienation.* New York: Doubleday, 1970.

Sedgwick, Eve Kosofsky. *The Coherence of Gothic Conventions.* New York: Methuen, 1986.

Shapiro, Barbara J. *Probability and Certainty in Seventeenth-Century England.* Princeton, N.J.: Princeton University Press, 1983.

Siebers, Tobin. *The Romantic Fantastic.* Ithaca, N.Y.: Cornell University Press, 1984.

Starr, George A. *Defoe and Spiritual Autobiography,* 1965. New York: Gordian Press, 1971.

Stock, R. D. *The Holy and the Daemonic from Sir Thomas Browne to William Blake.* Princeton, N.J.: Princeton University Press, 1982.

Sullivan, Jack. *Elegant Nightmares: The English Ghost Story from Le Fanu to Blackwood.* Athens: Ohio University Press, 1978.

Summers, Montague. *The Vampire: His Kith and Kin.* London: Routledge and Kegan Paul, 1928.

Thomas, Keith. *Religion and the Decline of Magic.* New York: Scribner's, 1975.

Thompson, G. R., ed. *The Gothic Imagination: Essays in Dark Romanticism.* Pullman: Washington State University Press, 1974.

Todorov, Tzvetan. *The Fantastic: A Structural Approach to a Literary Genre,* trans. Richard Howard, 1970. Ithaca, N.Y.: Cornell University Press, 1975.

———. "The Typology of Detective Fiction." In *The Poetics of Prose,* trans. Richard Howard. Ithaca, N.Y.: Cornell University Press, 1977.

Varma, Devendra P. *The Gothic Flame,* 1957. New York: Russell and Russell, 1966.

Varnado, S. L. "The Idea of the Numinous in Gothic Literature." In G. R. Thompson, ed., *The Gothic Imagination: Essays in Dark Romanticism.* Pullman: Washington State University Press, 1974.

Veeder, William R. *Mary Shelley and* Frankenstein: *The Fate of Androgyny.* Chicago: University of Chicago Press, 1986.

Vinaver, Eugene. *The Rise of Romance.* New York: Oxford University Press, 1971.

Walker, D. P. *The Decline of Hell: Seventeenth-Century Discussions of Eternal Torment.* London: Routledge and Kegan Paul, 1964.

Wasserman, Earl R. *The Subtler Language: Critical Readings of Neoclassic and Romantic Poems.* Baltimore, Md.: Johns Hopkins University Press, 1959.
Watt, Ian. *The Rise of the Novel,* 1957. Berkeley: University of California Press, 1962.

Articles

Claridge, Laura P. "Parent-Child Tensions in *Frankenstein:* The Search for Communion." *Studies in the Novel,* 17, 1 (1985), 14–26.
Coats, Daryl R. "Bram Stoker and the Ambiguity of Identity." In *Publications of the Mississippi Philological Association,* n.v. (1984), 88–105.
Demetrakopoulos, Stephanie. "Feminism, Sex Role Exchanges, and Other Subliminal Fantasies in Bram Stoker's *Dracula." Frontiers: Journal of Women's Studies,* 2, 3 (1977), 104–13.
Eggenschwiler, David. *"Melmoth the Wanderer:* Gothic on Gothic," *Genre,* 8 (1975), 165–81.
Fish, Stanley. "Literature in the Reader: Affective Stylistics," *New Literary History,* 2, 1 (1970), 123–62.
Fontana, Ernest. "Lombroso's Criminal Man and Stoker's *Dracula, Victorian Newsletter,* 66 (1984), 25–27.
Fradin, Joseph I. " 'The Absorbing Tyranny of Every-day Life': Bulwer-Lytton's *A Strange Story," Nineteenth-Century Fiction,* 16 (1961), 1–16.
Gibson, Walker. "Authors, Speakers, Readers, and Mock Readers," *College English,* 11 (1950), 265–69.
Goldberg, M. A. "Moral and Myth in Mrs. Shelley's *Frankenstein," Keats-Shelley Journal,* 8 (1959), 27–38.
Haggerty, George E. "Fact and Fancy in the Gothic Novel," *Nineteenth-Century Fiction,* 39, 4 (1985), 379–91.
Hennelly, Mark M., Jr. *"Dracula:* The Gnostic Quest and the Victorian Wasteland," *English Literature in Transition,* 20 (1977), 13–26.
Hirsch, Gordon D. "The End of the Gothic." Session on Gothic Fiction in Britain, MLA Convention. Washington, 29 Dec. 1984.
Jameson, Fredric. "Magical Narratives: Romance as Genre," *New Literary History,* 7 (1975), 135–63.
Johnson, Barbara. "My Monster / My Self," *Diacritics,* 12, 2 (1982), 2–10.
MacGillivray, Royce. *"Dracula:* Bram Stoker's Spoiled Masterpiece," *Queen's Quarterly,* 79 (1972), 518–27.
McInerney, Peter. *"Frankenstein* and the Godlike Science of Letters," *Genre,* 13 (1980), 455–75.
Null, Jack. "Structure and Theme in *Melmoth the Wanderer," Papers on Language and Literature,* 13 (1977), 136–47.
Prince, Gerald. "Introduction to the Study of the Narratee," *Poetique,* 14 (1973), 177–96.
Randel, Fred V. *"Frankenstein,* Feminism, and the Intertextuality of Mountains," *Studies in Romanticism,* 23, 4 (1984), 515–32.
Roth, Phyllis A. "Suddenly Sexual Women in Bram Stoker's *Dracula," Literature and Psychology,* 27 (1977), 113–21.
Seed, David. "The Narrative Method of *Dracula," Nineteenth-Century Fiction,* 40, 1 (1985), 61–75.
Senf, Carol A. *"Dracula:* The Unseen Face in the Mirror," *Journal of Narrative Technique,* 9 (1979), 160–70.
Tater, Maria. "The Houses of Fiction: Toward a Definition of the Uncanny," *Comparative Literature,* 33 (1981), 167–82.
Wall, Geoffrey. " 'Different from Writing': *Dracula* in 1897," *Literature and History,* 10, 1 (1984), 15–23.

Index

DUE DATE

BUR MAY 1 0 1988			
OCT 1 6 1992	OCT 2 1 REC'D		
BUR MAR 2 8 1996			
GL/Ree MAR 2 9 1996			
APR 1 7 2001			
APR 1 2 2001			
MAY 1 0 2001			
MAY 0 9 2001			
DEC 0 7 2006			
201-6503		Printed in USA